Schooling, the Puritan Imperative, and the Molding of an American National Identity

Education's "Errand Into the Wilderness"

Studies in Curriculum Theory
WILLIAM F. PINAR, Series Editor

Schooling, the Puritan Imperative, and the Molding of an American National Identity

Education's "Errand Into the Wilderness"

DOUGLAS McKNIGHT
University of Alabama

 LAWRENCE ERLBAUM ASSOCIATES, PUBLISHERS
2003   Mahwah, New Jersey   London

Lawrence Erlbaum Associates, Inc., Publishers
10 Industrial Avenue
Mahwah, NJ 07430

Cover illustration by Jeanette McKnight.
Cover design by Kathryn Houghtaling Lacey.

Library of Congress Cataloging-in-Publication Data

McKnight, Douglas.
Schooling, the Puritan imperative, and the molding of an American national identity : education's "errand into the wilderness" / Douglas McKnight.
    p.   cm.
   ISBN 0–8058–4317–5
   1. Moral education—United States. 2. Education—Aims and objectives—United States. 3. National characteristics, American. I. Title.
LC311 .M24 2003
370.11'4—dc21   2002035396

To Boo and Little Man.
Your errand awaits . . .

Contents

Preface

WE AGAIN HEAR AND SEE the jeremiads reverberate across the airwaves. We read them in editorials and scholarly works. They issue forth from both pulpit and podium. The ritual of crisis has begun, and it sounds something like this: Present-day America is perceived as immersed in a moral crisis due to certain cultural conditions; national identity has fractured, resulting in a pervading sense of uncertainty and anxiety about the future; public schools, as institutions charged with preserving the sacred/secular symbolic identity of America and its world mission of running an "errand into the wilderness" and creating a "city upon the hill" (Miller, 1957) have failed and must be reformed; and, finally, only through education can America be saved from this current cultural predicament.

The rhetorical trajectory of this anxiety-ridden ritual, produced from a fear that the fantasy of a grand destiny is in danger, has a history that goes back to the colonial Puritans who settled in America during the early 17th century. This small but cohesive and coherent band of "errand" runners generated the culture of the New England Way, which eventually evolved into the Yankee and finally the American Way. Puritans inscribed on the American physical and intellectual landscape a symbolic narrative that assembled, as well as constrained, the possible ways of perceiving and embodying the American identity and the sense of sacred/secular historical mission attached to that identity.

The intent of this historical jeremiad is to explore these elements within the American psyche and inquire into some of the effects of the symbolism at different points in American history.

Chapter 1 considers symbolism in American culture in terms of the production of a sacred/secular national identity, as well as how the colonial Puritans' (the first American historians) version of history emerged to narrate and explain for all the trajectory of America's past, present, and future. In general, American historians, especially educational historians, have written *America* as a country with a sacred/secular mission continually threatened by the immoral behavior of its inhabitants. These historians operated from the rhetorical form of the old colonial Puritan jeremiad, which celebrated the ideal of a great destiny for America even as it warned of the dangers to the enterprise by the immoral behavior of individual Americans. For these historians, schooling played a pivotal role in passing on this condition. American historians, as explainers of symbols, determined that the task of the social studies in schools is to transmit this story.

With this background of understanding, I approach the rest of this project through a particular trajectory. Chapter 2 relates the colonial Puritan production of the symbols "the errand in the wilderness," as well as how Puritan leaders developed moral maps for each individual to follow to mature into one able to serve the cultural institutions. I look at how these symbols shaped the colonial Puritan moral structure, which gave form to a cultural identity that was eventually extended to a national identity. Chapter 3 expands the analysis to include the ritual of the jeremiad as a pragmatic operation by which the gift of the errand is perpetuated in and by educational institutions. The rhetorical structure of the jeremiad informed educational institutions and instruction in ways that continue to this day—especially through the appropriation of 16th-century arts master Peter Ramus' curriculum maps and pedagogical methods.

Chapter 4 moves ahead in time to the cusp of the 20th century and beyond to explore how the symbolism of the errand haunted and silently navigated the cultural shifts in America, leading to the expressed purposes and functions that would comprise mass public education. Although the 20th century may have perceived itself as secular, the underlying conditions and impulses were still quite religious, still seeking the mind of God, so to speak.

Chapter 5 extends the inquiry to the middle-class professional's adoption of technological discourse as the privileged language to be applied to institutional life throughout America, but specifically to school life, one that retained the Ramist underpinnings and served the political/spiritual desires of middle-class professions. The social and educational jeremiads written during this time—while preserving the colonial Puritan impulse to perceive America as having universal and historical importance, as well as preserving the rhetorical map by which these impulses would be expressed—began to shift away from the sacred/secular, figural metaphors able to forever broaden and shift as the material conditions of the American terrain shifted. Such metaphors were replaced with technological ones, which, of course, were not perceived as metaphors at all but as something real and, therefore, natural. In turn, such language had a great effect on how the symbols were interpreted and perpetuated in a way that threatened the ambiguity necessary for symbols to survive.

Chapter 6 traces certain thematic drifts of how the errand was perpetuated by focusing on an individual who participated in the middle-class professional errand by calling for schools to assume the role of moral inculcators on a mass scale. I discuss the life and thought of William Torrey Harris, U.S. Commissioner of Education throughout the 1890s, whose lineage goes back to the colonial Congregationalists and, who, therefore, shared in the Puritan vision of America. In 1875, Harris became the president of the National Education Association; earlier he was the superintendent of schools in St. Louis, MO, a post he maintained throughout. Harris provides us with a necessary microcosm to discuss not only the embodiment of the errand identity and rhetorical form (his writings were jeremiadic in form and intent), but also how that process fits into his rhetoric of the function of the public schools as a moral inculcator. Harris, in many ways, is a perfect example of the transition in the discourse of the errand. Few wrote more than Harris at this crucial point in American educational history about the role of education and its relation to the national identity and to history. He was the embodiment of the tension and contradictions that existed in the middle-class Protestant inheritors of the Puritan errand, as well as an example of how the Puritans constructed the means by which an individual would become an American "institutional individual." Although claiming the title of philosopher, Harris more importantly oversaw the institution of schooling as a bureaucratic and technocratic form propelled by the rise of urban, middle-class professionals.

Chapter 7 examines how the symbolic gift has again emerged in the current sense of a national identity crisis and how it operates through the kinds of jeremiads being written.

The Afterword reflects on the condition that while many of the discussants of the current sense of moral crisis seek solutions to turn America back to its "original" path, there is a problem not being addressed: Just how far can the errand go, given the current dominance of certain discourses that flatten the ambiguity needed to sustain a symbol and allow it to incorporate new meanings? In other words, has the errand runner finally collapsed from exhaustion, with no meaning left to give? This question becomes even more significant in light of the tragedy now known as 9/11 (September 11, 2001), the day terrorists slammed airplanes into the twin towers of the World Trade Center and into the Pentagon. After that day, Americans quickly grasped for any symbolic means available to express grief and to create national unity and identity. Interestingly, the phrase that caught on was "God bless America." No matter how much people claim that Church and State are or should be separate, it is a false claim. Many Americans still perceive their identity in terms of a New Jerusalem, a city upon the hill, a place chosen by God and given a mission, an "errand into the wilderness," even though such symbolic forms seem to have lost the kind of force and meaning necessary to be culturally relevant in a world in which America has actually become the most powerful and feared nation. And as evidenced by the growing proliferation of calls for character education in American schools, Americans still perceive schooling as the primary means of preserving this notion of the errand. Although the language employed may no longer involve colonial Puritan biblical language, even though character education programs tend to appropriate the old standby discourse of Protestant values, the impulses and the patriarchal meanings within the words remain the same: Schools must somehow save America's individuals from corrupting forces, forces that could disrupt the Grand March of history with America at the forefront.

ACKNOWLEDGMENTS

There are many I would like to acknowledge in this endeavor: First, Dr. William F. Pinar, whose intellectual and psychological mentoring and friendship over the course of many years I am just beginning to fully understand and appreciate; Naomi Silverman, Editor at Lawrence Erlbaum Associates, who saw the worth in this project and shepherded it through publication, for which I am grateful; The University of Alabama, which awarded me a Research Advisory Council grant, enabling the completion of this project; and Dr. Steven Triche, whose friendship and whose scholarship on Peter Ramus' connection to the colonial Puritans' symbolic narratives and American schooling I turned to again and again.

Immense appreciation goes to Leslie Zganjar McKnight, my comrade and love for nearly two decades, who read every word in the manuscript and whose journalistic skills found and corrected my grammatical and syntactical misadventures.

And finally, Søren Kierkegaard, my patron saint of existential dread, who continues to teach me each day that no matter how many words I use to seek truth, in the end I must eventually arrive at silence.

—Douglas McKnight

1

The Puritan Gift: The Historical Condition of Writing the Symbolic Narrative of America

There is ... a Latin proverb ... : —Nature, expelled with a pitchfork, ever returns. This proverb is exemplified by the history of symbolism. However you may endeavor to expel it, it ever returns. Symbolism is no mere idle fancy or corrupt degeneration: It is inherent in the very texture of human life. —*Whitehead (1927/1955, p. 61)*

Like all simple and unsophisticated people, we Americans have a sublime faith in education. Faced with any difficult problem of life, we set our minds at rest sooner or later by the appeal to the school. We are convinced that education is the one unfailing remedy for every ill to which man is subject. —*Counts (1969, p. 3)*

IN GENERAL, historical work on American education supplies little analysis of the colonial Puritans' place within the American educational model beyond a generalized comment: Puritans were the first European Americans to craft a compulsory school law in 1647 requiring all townships to instruct their children in the basics of writing and reading the Bible, for authoritarian and religious reasons rather than democratic ones (e.g., Curti, 1959; Sadovnik, Cookson & Semel, 2001; Spring, 1990; Welter, 1962). Beyond the Puritans' worth as a historical artifact, and even oddity, in American educational history, not much else is supplied, especially in terms of how the colonial Puritans' cultural productions may have affected the perceived purposes of education throughout American history.

The consensus seems to be that Puritan schooling was not about teaching democracy or freedom and liberty—educational ideals that appeared after the American Revolution and, therefore, apparently were not relevant to those studying contemporary education. In general, educational historians, especially revisionists (e.g., Ellis, 2001), asserted that before the American Revolution, education in America was primarily concerned with the development of a Godly life (Spring, 1986); that after the Revolution it became more about the development of an American national identity; that during the late 1800s and early 1900s, education reflected class conflict and so became the institution for socialization, control of knowledge, and sorting students into certain socioeconomic roles (e.g., Callahan, 1962; Katz, 1975, 1987; Shapiro & Purpel, 1993; Spring, 1989). The revisionists follow a Hegelian and Marxist historical and philosophical analysis, and, therefore, propose and impose a powerful interpretation on the historical purposes, effects, and development of American education. However, by depending on a Marxian analysis of class struggle, the whole pre-Revolution period of colonial history is simply dismissed as being about the teaching of religion and little more, with no artifacts worth excavating that would reveal some insight into the present condition of curriculum and pedagogy in America.

Although it is granted here that the ultimate purpose of schooling for the colonial Puritans possessed a decisively religious tone, such analysis ignores the value and power their discourse had on the American consciousness. It is certainly "reasonable" to conclude that colonial Puritans conceived the purpose of education, which includes the institution of school, as primarily the process of "Godly learning" (Morgan, 1988). However, "Godly learning" was far from a form of group religious fanaticism that denigrated secular knowledge in favor of pure faith. As part of the Reformation, Puritans followed Calvin's edict that each individual must enter into, participate, and be successful in the world in a way that would help fulfill the greater corporate mission of America, that of becoming a "city upon a hill."

The colonial Puritans inscribed on the national consciousness a sacred/secular symbolic narrative sending America on an "errand into the wilderness" to become a "city upon a hill." This narrative provided a national identity of sorts, a corporate historical teleology in which America would fulfill the role of New Israel. The Puritans also provided the rhetorical and institutional means of perpetuating this symbolic narrative: the crisis sermon—sometimes on sacred matters, sometimes on more mundane matters—called the *jeremiad*, written and spoken by reverend and teacher (who were often one and the same until the 1800s); and the institution of schooling, considered the moral and intellectual process of bringing the individual into the corporate fold and whose pedagogical methods mirrored the jeremiad form. These continue to this day. Indeed, much of the success of America's perceived world destiny has been dictated by a passionate faith in education (i.e., schooling), a faith that seems unquestioned to this day (Perkinson, 1991; and e.g., Cremins, 1964; Cuban & Shipps, 2000; Curti, 1959; Hirsch, 1987; Kliebard, 1987, 1992; Ravitch, 1985, 2000; Spring, 1972, 1989; Tanner, D., 1991; Tanner, L., 1982; Tanner & Tanner, 1980; Tyack, 1974, 1993; the list could be quite extensive). However, for historians of education, this faith in education and its connection to a national purpose never seems to trace back to the colonial Puritans.

Their role in creating for the nation a historical drama and the educational means to continue it seems unnoticed due to the assumption that the Puritans were merely concerned with theological truth and autocratic government. This categorization of the colonial Puritans is opposed to what are considered the "real" American ideals, freedom and democracy, with the federal civil government existing to protect and further those ideals. However, this binary opposition serves to mask the colonial Puritans' own rhetorical forms that created the symbolic narrative and that actually began the process of linguistic secularization that became fully privileged during the 1800s (Bercovitch, 1975, 1993).

Even though the language shifted from America as God's chosen place (still heard from pulpit and political soapbox to this day) to America as "leader of the free world" or engaged in Manifest Destiny or in the liberation of "oppressed" (i.e., not democratic or capitalist) countries, the impulse first expressed through colonial Puritan jeremiads still haunts the national consciousness. There exists a fervent hope in a historical, national purpose of transcendence for America, as well as a fear that this mission will be derailed, and a faith in education as the institutional means to protect from such a failure.

From this perspective, America possesses an unusual and unique blend of the sacred and the secular in that it is the only nation in which "nationalism carries with it the Christian meaning of the sacred.... Of all symbols of identity, only America has united nationality and universality, civic and spiritual selfhood, secular and redemptive history, the country's past and paradise to be, in a single synthetic ideal" (Bercovitch, 1978, p. 176). However, for such a condition to persevere, a founding symbolic narrative must be presented as a natural outcome of history and must be written on the American landscape through the stories it tells about itself. An explanation is symbolism:

> A symbol is something which has value not only because of its content, but because it can be produced—i.e. because it is a document by means of which the members of a community recognize one another; whether it is a religious symbol or appears in a secular context . . . in every case the meaning of the symbolism depends on its physical presence and a representational function only by being shown or spoken. (Gadamer, 1993, pp. 72–73)

For America, symbolic phrases and narratives of "errand into the wilderness" and "city upon a hill" became the historical documents to articulate America's representation of itself to the world.

In America, historians have not only participated fully in the assumptions of America having a destiny, but they also have been at the forefront of retelling, explaining, and defining such symbolic characterizations of America. Historian Arthur Schlesinger, Jr., is almost militaristic in his rendition of the importance of history to America's perceived purpose: "History is a weapon. Who controls the meaning and understanding of a nation's history controls the future" (1991a, p. 52). Schlesinger's comment represents another important point concerning the symbolic narrative and how it is perpetuated. Even within such a short statement, one can detect an urgent sense of crisis. His statement is more than the outcome of historical analysis. It is a warning and an exhortation all rolled into one. In other words, it emerges out of the old colonial Puritan cultural jeremiads that extolled the virtues of the "city upon a hill," warned of the immoral actions of individuals threatening the great mission, and exhorted all in the congregation to embody the virtues that ensure success. Simply, American historians are the first ones to participate in the jeremiad ritual of the crisis when it is perceived that something, usually the moral failing of the country's inhabitants, is causing the great "errand" to decay. They are also the first ones to point toward education as the means to revive the great "errand."

A good example of this is the National Council for the Social Studies (NCSS) presidential address by Michael Hartoonian (1996), historian and then president of the NCSS, who penned an educational jeremiad that would have heartened the old Puritan firebrand and jeremiad writer, Cotton Mather. Hartoonian's warning and exhortation addressed the moral failings of individuals and the continued obligation of schools, especially history teachers, to remind Americans of their historical mission:

> There is little disagreement today that the republic is in trouble. Our collective lives lack moral strength: our infra-structure needs a complete update; our social institutions need nurturing, renewed purpose, ethical leadership. . . . Above all else, we seem to lack the courage for rightful behavior." (p. 3–4)

For Hartoonian and other public social studies and historical entities, schools are charged with moral/cultural enculturation and transmission. The logic goes like this: Fix public schools by reviving their "original" charge—the imposition on the young, understood as existing within a malleable state that can be manipulated and changed, of a particular American morality. Key to this original charge is the use of history as a means to inform and guide the individual to an institutional identity based on history. The belief is that history must take a priority in American education or America's purpose as a "light upon the world" will be threatened.

Part of this process is to instruct students in the symbolic narrative of America, specifically its historical tale of redemption and transcendence. This has been the call of the historian from the first histories written by the colonial Puritans, and it has been the charge for those developing the first history textbooks in schools during the early 1800s (Schwartz, 2001). In fact, such symbolic narratives, even as they moved from religious thought to more civil, economic, and secular meanings, have persevered due to the nature of symbolic narratives.

Symbolism relies on two seemingly opposing forces: disruptions and social crises that emerge in historical times to which symbols must react and change to survive; and particular national institutions, which at their core are based on the belief that American institutions stand outside history and serve as the means by which the symbolic and moral expressions are spread. In other words, for symbols to sustain a grasp on a nation's consciousness, there must exist certain psychological events, such as a ritualized crisis. These events, expressed through public jeremiad activity, function to elevate the symbolic narrative, in this case America having an "errand into the wilderness," from the unconscious to the conscious so that it can preserve its flexibility to adapt and survive changing material conditions. At the same time, this public ritual discusses and presents to all the moral identity that is supposed to be the concrete expression of the symbols. Most generally, this identity, believed to give America a coherent past and sense of purpose, has historically emerged out of the categories White, Protestant, nuclear family, middle class, and loyal to the economic and religious ways of the country produced 300 years ago.

For the most part, this highly charged drama has played itself out in the form of editorials, popular and academic books, and vocal public cries for public schools to inculcate students into "traditional American morality." In this, a direct correspondence is made between this notion of American morality as imparted in the early years of schooling and the preservation of national identity. In other words, the moral fabric of Americans determines national identity. What follows from this way of thinking is that if the moral forms as inherited lose coherence, then the national identity—America as holding a special place in secular and spiritual history—is lost forever (Bercovitch, 1978, 1993; Grob & Billias, 1972; Noble, 1965; Tyack, 1993). As Noble (1965) argued, American historians, though changing the content of their language, have continued as the

> chief spokesman for this cultural tradition. From 1830 to the present, each generation has seen the emergence of a historian who has become a public philosopher . . . [who preserves] the traditions of the first Englishmen who came to establish a New England. (pp. 4–5)

A means to provide insight into how this unique American condition was extended from the Puritans onward is to suggest a thematic narrative, or better, a metaphor for the American process of writing history. This metaphor supplies a structure to better understand how the Puritans developed a symbolic narrative that was protected and carried forth by later historians of America, especially by historians of American education, as well as schools beginning with the very first Puritans. The metaphor is history as a symbolic gift, one wrapped in irony and ambiguity. The notion of a gift also offers a perspective as to why this symbolic narrative has become problematic, and for good or bad, no longer as powerful as it once was.

THE GIFT

The Puritans offered the future a gift: a symbolic identity, America, and a national purpose, the symbol of the errand into the wilderness. However, in a style that wedded the literal and the figural, ambiguity haunts every word produced by the Puritans, despite the persistent attempt by each Puritan individual to interpret from the Bible the exact method by which to attain moral certitude. Puritans privileged the written text, with each congregation expected to sustain a high rate of literacy. The Puritans supplied their cultural inheritors, the urban Protestant American professional middle class of the late 19th century, with a host of cultural documents by which to read and embody Puritan moralistic impulses. However, this gift came at a price. Within the long historical tradition of giving exists a plethora of demands, responsibilities, and expectations of reciprocity. A gift can never be given nor received in complete freedom or with certainty of meaning.

The colonial Puritan gift was a particular kind of rhetoric of symbolism, even a symbolic gesture or language constructed from and pointed toward concerns of morality, interests that compelled later generations to view time and identity in socially redemptive ways. This gift began the process of American identity construction and was part of a particular type of economy of exchange. Through this rhetorical symbol, the past is folded into the present: The gift is the present, the presentation of the past in a contemporary moment, in which certain possibilities of future thought and action will be constructed. This notion of giving, of history as a gift, attempts to operate from several different recognitions simultaneously. A brief etymological tracing illustrates the ambiguity of such a notion, of how it functions to construct "identity" even as a history of the gift is constructed:

> Gift n. about 1250, thing given or a present. . . . Middle Dutch gift (modern Dutch gift, meaning poison) and . . . Old High German *gihfte,* (poison). . . . The meaning of poison, found in modern Dutch and German . . . is also a specialization of meaning similar to Late Latin *dosis* and Greek *dosis,* dose of medicine, drug. (*BDE;* Barnhardt, 1988, p. 431)

The gift is not only something given, which implies that the other is pleased to receive it, and as such has the curative effect of medicine; the gift also acts as a poison that can infect the one receiving the gift. Or sometimes the medicine heals an ailment, but in interacting with other medicines produces other ill effects. At the same time, the disease's cure is often an appropriate amount of the poison. For instance, Salk injected himself with polio virus and found that the virus held the components necessary for the cure. Creative and destructive possibilities exist simultaneously in the notion of the gift.

In terms of the Puritan symbology, the gift operates in this way: Those who receive the symbol, a uniquely crafted American identity blessed with a teleology in sacred and secular history, receive a present rich in cultural sources and possibilities by which to draw from and live life in America. One can pull meaning and purpose from the Puritan symbols of America and the errand into the wilderness. One also must reciprocate. In turn one must agree to embody America as a sacred/ secular representation of the Puritan symbol of the errand into the wilderness and the particular identities that emerge from this symbol. One must forsake certain resources of non-American cultural identities and purposes (i.e., as was expected of immigrants, and of freedmen and southerners after the Civil War). And, one must be willing to present the gift in perpetuity, by infusing children with the intellectual and emotional bonds that emerged from the symbolic construction.

Within the gift is a demand that we forever return home to the ways of the giver, to give in to our symbolic progenitor. In the gift is a lesson in how to go about living one's life so that the gift will be eternalized. This gift not only sets the conditions for understanding national identity (and so the political act of writing history), but also produces a peculiarly American impulse to operate along two historical narrative trajectories that are not mutually exclusive and that fit within the Puritan impulse. The historian moves toward "saving" the world from its non-American ways by writing the story of America as a natural outcome of historical and dialectical forces. In the other, the historian writes to return America, through the lessons culled from historical scholarship, to an "original" historical intent of America as a culmination of forces outside history. This America was that of a more perfect union, an ahistorical symbol that is secure by means of moral behavior (Bercovitch, 1978, 1993). In other words, the historian writes America as either transcending or attempting to transcend history.

EXPLORING THE ECONOMY OF THE GIFT

Instead of studying the institution of education as if it arose in some hermetic isolation, separate from American cultural history, I focus more on relationships among the abstract notion "America," national identity, individual identity, and public education's function within this nexus of concepts. From this has emerged an emphasis on symbolic constructions and the way those living in particular historical eras cohere around and find value in such cultural symbols to express and make sense of their condition.

In other words, what Puritan symbols provided the urban middle-class American Protestants in the late 19th century with a framework by which to address this impulse toward understanding national identity as a reflection of themselves? In what ways did this belief guide them to construct public education as the mechanism to preserve the present, and so the future, of the errand and of national identity? How did these ways function to flatten out and reduce such symbols to the point that the symbols no longer operate as intended by the Puritans?

To address the errand, one does not begin with the past but with the present. The questioner, the interpreter, has a responsibility to turn and face himself or herself and reveal all residue of the gift. This exposes an irony in the very act of asking certain questions. For if the writing of American history is as presented here, then I, participating in some form of historical narrative, must also participate in the economy of the symbolic gift. In no way can I separate myself from the language and symbols I have inherited. In effect, this forces my writing to operate within its domain; language is my only means by which to mediate and represent. This does not mean I am a passive receptor. I appropriate language and have the flexibility to produce meanings as much as reveal meanings. This historical narrative is an interpretative, rhetorical device by which to participate in the gift of the errand even while attempting to burrow new paths within the inherited linguistic sediment in a way that reveals how this unique American symbolic structure has produced and affected the notion of education.

This interpretation is a negotiation between my own productions of meaning as I write my own tale of American educational history and revealed meaning, rather than the human science orientation in which meaning is simply revealed (Scholes, 1989). What has developed consists of something of a double movement, one that operates from a recognition that there comes a time when one must again question the inherited symbols and decide whether to discard or revitalize them, especially in the field of education, a field wholly wrapped in the assumptions of the errand. Of course, a caveat to such a statement is the possibility that we really have no control over either; that the best we can do is to "re-cognize" the whole symbolic structure. One could call it, as Adams (1918/1974) discovered in his writing of *The Education of Henry Adams,* the irony that history holds against the historian.

First, as I began to work through the discourse of history, I had a recognition similar to that of Adams. I realized that I am also a child of that language, a language that by its very nature restricts my expression to certain syntactical structures. These patterns tend to perpetuate symbolic meanings meditated on even in the process of questioning the value of the received symbols. The language predetermines, to a large extent, the questions asked and the answers given. However, it is crucial that one questions.

In the jeremiads, a form of rhetorical writing that schooled, exhorted, and encouraged even as it warned and threatened of doom, colonial Puritan clergy implored each congregation to always question and contemplate the value, the morality, of an act. In an acknowledgment of the economy of the gift, what takes place in the following pages is a historical jeremiad questioning the usefulness of the jeremiad ritual of exhorting Americans ever onward and upward in their errand into the wilderness. A definition of this ritual is in order. Basically, a jeremiad is a form of writing, a mix of prophecy, history, and biblical and moral excursions into the difficulty of determining right and wrong. The jeremiad evolved primarily as a ritualistic discourse to remind individuals and communities that morality was the root of earthly existence. These writings, which intensified when a crisis was perceived (or constructed), translated colonial Puritan identity into a broader, more abstract, American identity. With such transcendence firmly in his or her mind, the jeremiad writer proceeded to warn of God's wrath if this connection between God, self, community, and the nation ever unraveled.

However, the jeremiad was not just about the probability of impending doom. I say doom because the Puritans, in their own complex way, believed in the basic depravity of humans; they lived with the disturbing realization that they would always fall short of any ideal. They lived their lives within the tension of this paradox. The jeremiads also celebrated the historical and sacred opportunity believed to be possessed by the Puritans because they were, as they continually attested to in their writings, God's new chosen. To preserve that "chosenness," through the act of moral contemplation, meant possible salvation for those maintaining that identity. The burden of God's plan was on them (Bercovitch, 1975, 1978; Brumm, 1970; Miller, 1957).

For the first American Puritans, those who followed John Winthrop in 1630 on board the *Arbella,* success of this plan depended on their ability to educate their children, and later, as the symbol of the errand into the wilderness was extended, to educate the rest.

Only through one's ability to read and interpret the Bible could one reveal, or be enlightened to, the correct moral action, an action that would first and foremost preserve the coherence of the community. With the first irony always looking over my shoulder, I appropriate the words of Bendetto Croce: "Every true history is contemporary history" (quoted in Grob & Billias, 1972, p. 1). Within this is an acknowledgment of the impossibility of getting behind the symbols to reveal an essential reality about America or enacting a political policy that would return America to its "authentic" state of existence as the light of the world. To reveal a myth as a myth only takes place through the construction of another myth. As Percy (1991) said, and I paraphrase: We are symbol mongerers, for symbols are all that we have. The creation and preservation of symbols are human impulses; even those symbols that we claim are no longer symbols, but pure reflections of literal reality. Symbols allow human possibilities to become expressed in the world. We function in the world through symbolic perception. Early 20th century philosopher Alfred North Whitehead identified this human tendency. He argued in a series of lectures in 1927 that humanity had to employ symbols to express itself. Acting on or producing symbolism is not an idle masquerade to escape from or ignore some actual truth behind the mask, in which "real" is hidden. Instead, symbols provide a fluid structure by which meaning can emerge and be applied by human beings to the world (Whitehead, 1927/1955).

I differ with Whitehead's notion of symbolic operations of acting in the world in this: It is my contention that, although symbols may point to something much older and may contain impulses harbored by humankind for ages, such impulses are not primordial in the sense that they reveal the essence of all life. They are not the ultimate transcendental signifiers (Caputo, 1987). We go forth in life without a world full of any deep, underlying truth to guide us. We operate from a nexus of symbols that can but provide meaning in a way that enables us to function compassionately in a world without a priori or transcendental guideposts (Caputo, 1987; Rorty, 1976; Scholes, 1989).

It is impossible to "know" the past because of ambiguity and opaqueness of language, and because of the problem presented by a person experiencing time and place by way of multiple perspectives. Even by means of a *cinéma vérité* one cannot "know" history, for that relies on a belief that reality is fully in view if one just has all the angles covered and can locate the "correct" language by which to pin it down and explain it. This assumption has guided philosophical thought for centuries (Rorty, 1976). It is a kind of thought that American historians of education, as well as those involved in educational research, theory, and practice, have generally participated in: an embedded belief that meaning is universal, continuous, and receptive to language's direct touch. This is problematic, if not false.

Yet, language is crucial, if not inescapable. Language emerges out of and provides the contours and necessary inclusions and exclusions of meaning characterized by each individual's inner experiences, however they are structured, as each individual comes in contact with others having their own grouping of inner experiences and understandings. In other words, language does not directly represent knowledge; it constructs it (Percy, 1991). Language supplies an indirect means to communicate these experiences, and allows us to string together groups of concepts that can provide us meanings that do not and cannot exist outside engaging in such an activity. Due to the inherent opaqueness of language, one must be sensitive to how certain linguistic notions emerge and cohere into a symbolic structure. This structure is by no means solid or stable in a way that makes one think of a foundation built on concrete blocks. Instead, it is porous in that it seeps up from a deep deposit of symbolic possibilities, which congregate within the structure's parameters in a way that infuses it with the necessary vitality (Wittgenstein, 1973). This process, both exclusionary and inclusionary, advances through time due to the very historical disruptions that would threaten the symbolic structure's integrity, causing it to disperse.

Within the discontinuities of history—those moments of actual social disruptions and changes that shift the face of America into something empirically different from what it was before—is preserved a cultural faith in Progress (in God or Spirit), faith in a historical purpose as generated by the Puritan symbolism of America. An irony is that even though over time the Puritans became characterized as fanatical radicals, blamed for all the "bad" aspects of the American past because of their supposed intolerance, Puritan symbology has been hard at work. This symbology persevered and even prospered, even as many Americans in later centuries decried the colonial Puritans.

NO ESCAPE FROM THE SYMBOLS

To sustain certain symbols, such as America and errand into the wilderness, their meanings must continually be made current even as the material practices change due to the day-to-day interactions that create new events and demand new responses.

As briefly addressed earlier, the field of American history participates in this renewal ritual, even as it remains dependent on the provisions of traditional philosophy (the possibility of a universal knowledge that can reduce inherited symbolism to having one particular meaning that can be revealed). At the turn of the 20th century, alternative philosophies of language and knowledge arose but were not appropriated. These theories describe the workings of language and how human beings can "understand" each other at a time when a priori knowledge categories no longer seem to carry such currency. Simply, no two people ever have the same experience of a phenomenon, for each brings to that event a prior constellation of thoughts, experiences, and understandings different from the other. Whitehead (1927/1955) provided a useful way to explain this operation:

> Also in its flux a symbol will have different meanings for different people. At any epoch some people have the dominant mentality of the past, some of the present, others of the future, and others of the many problematic futures which will never dawn. . . . If two nations speak the same language, this emotional efficacy of words and phrases will in general differ for the two.
>
> What is familiar for one nation will be strange for the other nation; what is charged with intimate associations for the one is empty for the other. For example, if the two nations are somewhat widely sundered, with a different fauna and flora, the nature-poetry of one nation will lack its complete directness of appeal to the other nation. (pp. 63, 67)

Language becomes the necessary means to communicate those individual understandings, even though language can never directly represent the experience. Language can only point. Or better, language can only indicate (Derrida, 1973). Over time, in communal interaction, these linguistic indications go through a process of comparison. Out of this process emerges a broad spectrum of particular types of symbolic though contingent structures in the community. These contingent structures provide the constellations of possible meanings and understandings in terms of how the community comes to perceive and identify itself in terms of the cosmos, the earth, the community, and each individual (Wittgenstein, 1973).

The resulting linguistic symbols tend to adhere to other groupings in a way that produces a symbolic structure for a particular community. This structure not only falls together in a way that elicits certain responses, actions, thoughts, and meanings, but is malleable in that it shifts its contours and incorporates new meanings that arise out of people's day-to-day interaction with the world. Through their material practices and habits of immediate living, people operate out of certain inherited family resemblances. But when these resemblances begin to lose the loose coherence that maintains their symbolic meanings, they must be readjusted and revitalized. This process of restructuring a new set of possible meanings incorporated within a symbol succeeds when it also preserves certain functions and impulses that led to the construction of particular symbols in the first place. Otherwise, the symbolic structure collapses.

This process of preserving symbolic structures, producing again meanings that arrange around certain indications and assumptions and impulses of a community and the community's sense of itself, is a ritual process. It is through the ritual, engaged in by American historians and institutionalized in public education, that the symbols are preserved even as the meanings shift and are negotiated.

An essential activity in the life of symbols is the process of mediation and interpretation (Stivers, 1994). Whitehead (1927/1955) furnished a useful statement on how this takes place:

[L]anguage binds a nation together by the common emotions which it elicits, and is yet the instrument whereby freedom of thought and individual criticism finds its expression. . . . The state depends in a very particular way upon the prevalence of symbols which combine direction to some well-known course of action with some deeper reference to the purpose of state. The self-organization of society depends on commonly diffused symbols evoking common diffused ideas, and at the same time indicating commonly understood actions. (pp. 68, 76)

An effect of the Protestant Reformation was an intensified emphasis placed on the importance of the written text. A reason for this was Calvin's insistence that the individual had a duty to read the Bible for himself or herself to directly receive God's wisdom and truth. Education became important in terms of learning to read the Bible, instead of passively receiving the word as a mysterious missive delivered by a priest. Education became the act of revealing to one's self the moral path to take in a depraved world. Because it was recognized that the written word was ambiguous, interpretation became extremely important for those groups arising out of the Protestant Reformation. Puritans, a Protestant group that emerged out of the Reformation and adhered to a strict form of Calvinism, were intensely interested in the development of interpretations. The Puritans were recognized as highly educated and literate. As such, they were viewed as dangerous, if not overzealous and harsh in their interpretations and their willingness to apply those interpretations to everyone and all things. Puritans wrote about everything.

Texts in Western civilization, due to the spread of books, literacy, and the philosophical legacies of truth representation, to a large degree provided the means through which the ritual of the jeremiad occurred. Hence, texts became the prime vehicle for public education as a harbinger of curricula. Simply, the Puritans were the most literate group to settle in America. They brought with them a coherent, well-developed sense of who they were and why they had come to America. They conceived of education and literacy as absolutely imperative for the development of self and community. Through extensive textual productions, and especially through the development of Cotton Mather's historical form (those who supply the narrative of history also supply the syntax from which meanings can emerge), the Puritans offered later historians and other public intellectuals concerned with the meaning of America a deep fund of documents and coherent tales by which to write about and interpret America as a Puritan fantasy.

Often these intellectuals, these political and religious radicals, were not aware that the methods and symbolic understandings they inherited had a built-in radar, so to speak, for the Puritan impulse. These writers sought meanings for America during times of crisis, specifically those times when Protestant middle-class Americans perceived a distinct absence of security. The Puritan gift offered them a way that would forever bring their children back to their own sacred/secular redemptive fantasy.

PURITAN HISTORICAL FORM

The Puritan historical form was unique. It arose out of a disruptive point in history when new metaphors could emerge that altered the dominant discourses. During the Protestant Reformation and its after-effects, Europe experienced a breadth of change that encompassed almost every facet of life and thought. The Puritans magnified and took advantage of the historical variation. They left the European continent, a physical and figural break from the past, so to speak. They left a "corrupt" civilization for what was given the metaphor of an empty desert or wilderness (Heimert, 1953). The wilderness was an empty space on which to inscribe their intentions. But a language is needed in order to inscribe. The Puritans recognized this and developed a discourse suitable for their sense of mission—a language that would guide them through the uncertainties that tend to erupt in times of great social turmoil and that would spell out to others the significance of their acts (Bercovitch, 1993; Brumm, 1970; Miller, 1953, 1957).

The Puritans created a language that confounded the formal categories of rhetoric and history. They produced a symbolically engaged discourse born of a marriage between sacred and prophetic history and a realist, literal rendering of human existence popularized by the efforts of those involved with the Protestant Reformation. The new narrative retained vestiges of each form. It was not a product of some dialectical transcendence, but a conflation of scripture and literal historical events presented as "reality" and preordained in the theological and secular spheres. Bercovitch (1975, 1978) explored the hold that the New England Puritan interpretive mode had on later American historians, poets, and social thinkers on the notion of national identity. He wrote of the Puritans' complex, sometimes even tortured, logic that relied on the flexibility of certain symbols to sustain their habits of thought as representative of the American culture:

> In short, beginning with America, they recast the whole dead secular world in their own image. The image required confirmation through

· what we would now call symbolic interpretation. The New England colonist not only had a private vision to convey, he had to convey it in metaphors that overturned the conventions from which those metaphors arose. (1975, p. 13)

Bercovitch (1975) continued:

In retrospect, it seems safe to say that such descriptions [the Puritan sacred/secular histories] represent the process of the creation of the symbol of America. But the theocracy's entire rationale hinged on their being read hermeneutically, as a record of figural facts rather than as mere spiritualizations or hyperbole. Early New England rhetoric is a titanic effort to secularize the traditional images without abandoning the claims of the exegesis. (p. 14)

The Puritans, through their jeremiadic histories, an important rhetorical vehicle, had to convince the Old World that America was the culmination of God's literal and figural plan. The effect of this Puritan form of "history," or better, symbolic narrative, characterized by Mather's *Magnalia Christi Americana* (1702/1853), was to invest the founding of New England, a material, historical event, with a figural, Biblical import. American identity was linked with sacred identities as presented in the Bible. This was a soteriological, Christological, historical tale. *Soteriological,* according to Bercovitch (1978), is the theological doctrine of salvation effected by Christ (literally meaning to save); *Christological,* the study of Christ's person and qualities so that one can become a visible saint.

This method of interpretation and narrative presentation constructed a particular perspective of American identity that gave priority to the Puritan impulse to present New England as the core of America. In turn, America was converted into God's chosen place; the Puritans became God's elect flock, chosen to fulfill the earthly prophecy necessary to make possible the day of God's judgment and the new reign of Christ on earth. Such a grand impulse, or even strategy, did not degrade or lose its potency in the late 1800s. It continued even as historical techniques multiplied into a wide range of variations: from narrative, interpretive, literary histories, such as those represented by Parkman, who developed a celebratory form of history, to the so called 20th-century social scientific histories operating from wholly "realist" and "literal" evidential forms and methods that formalized the differentiation between rhetoric and literal historical accounts, two forms that the Puritans never found need to separate.

Although the colonial Puritan language employed to perpetuate the figural sense of American identity as having sacred/secular redemptive purpose became submerged in the mid-19th century, the impulse to perceive American identity along that trajectory did not dissipate. This, as Geertz (1973) pointed out, speaks to the strong influence of the sacred/ secular symbolic marriage even when historians or anthropologists dismiss such symbolism as unrealistic or not affecting the material social-structural processes of a culture.

In fact, one could argue that the assumptions compelling Mather's explicit rendering of America as a New England production became more dominant after the late 1800s when they became implicit assumptions about America's national identity and its "natural" position in the world and in world history. Instead of history as soteriology or Christology, 19th-century American writers, when speaking of the American present and future, gazed less at the heavens and more at the material conditions of the physical landscape as a way to attain the ideal in the present although not in the future.

A certain religious zeal was evident, even in such a secular, technological framework. Instead of Christ coming to reign through the efforts of America as a nation, the language now presented America as the "light of the world" in terms of its democracy, its economic status, and its military power. "American scripture" (Maier, 1997) was still linked to the Protestant interpretation of the Bible, but now filtered through Enlightenment documents such as the Declaration of Independence and the Constitution. These documents perpetuated the sense that only in America, and only through American efforts, could earthly social ills find solutions. These assumptions were provided by the first American historians, the Puritans, with the effect of embedding in the New England consciousness a faith in the redemptive purpose of the New World. From these beginning points, an entire constellation of historical thoughts gathered.

INHERITING HISTORY:
FROM PATRICIANS TO PROFESSIONALS

If the 17th century saw the emergence of a new function for historical writing developed by the Puritans, the 19th and 20th centuries saw a shift from emphasizing the sacred sense of history to a more overtly secular, or better, a technological understanding.

History at this time was perceived as another branch of literature calculated to reach as broad an audience as possible. However, the Puritan notion of American destiny, and the warnings of what would happen if America turned away, ran throughout the writings of men such as Francis Parkman, George Bancroft, Washington Irving, and William Prescott. These men believed that through the literary technique, inspired by the Romantic era, they could reveal the general, universal truths that lay beneath a surface distorted by the flow of history. For the Patricians, history had a Hegelian bent. There was the general assumption by American historians at this time (as well as by English historians) that history was a grand deterministic, dialectical, and rational operation leading events progressively to a final culminating Utopia on earth.

This philosophy of history arose out of Hegel's philosophy of Spirit, which can be generally called a philosopher's God. Spirit was translated from the German *Geist* (spirit, ghost, intellect, mind). This type of history had as its stated intent the need to explain the essential nature of the historical subject. It was believed that such an explanation could be arrived at by a particular method that operated from an assumption; a literal copy of the past through close inspection of documents could be rendered. This method was transported from Germany into some of the more prominent American universities in the last days of the 19th century (Novik, 1988). These assumptions had the effect of revealing the present as natural, predetermined, and, as such, an admirable circumstance, or at least a condition, if riddled with social ills, that would cure itself as the dialectical function of history progressed. Simply, change equaled progress (Bowers, 1987). The Patricians in America felt it their responsibility to deliver this gospel to all Americans. As Grob and Billias (1972) wrote, in many ways these Patricians carried forward the Puritan torch of destiny:

> Running through their writings were three basic themes: the idea of progress.... [T]he movement toward more liberty in world history; and the idea of mission—that the United States had a special designate to serve as a model of a free people to the rest of the world in leading the way to a more perfect life. This last theme, in effect, was nothing more than a restatement of the idea of mission first set forth by the Puritan historians. (p. 5)

From the beginning, the tale that became "history" in America has had the effect of locating historians in a flight of thought that has functioned to preserve institutions. Even radical-minded historians called not for the end of the institutions that controlled historical thought, but for reform so that the institutions could "recapture" their former purity (Higham, 1990):

> During the seventeenth century the . . . history was written by Puritan Clergymen and by lay officials associated with them in creating a new Zion in the wilderness. . . . Their history was a further extension of scripture: a chronicle of God's inscrutable will working within their own community. . . . The professional historian materialized in the guise of a teacher-specialist. After a long intervening period of free-lance scholarship, historians again became, as they had been in Puritan New England, servants of an institution. (pp. 4–5)

Other patterns of thought, or possible loose categories, produced or characterized by assumptions about the nature of history, emerged in the late 19th and early 20th centuries in America. This era saw the advent of professional historians, and the emergence of history departments within certain elite universities. Coinciding with this shift in who would write the histories of America were the kinds of theories that these new historians would apply. The trajectory of thought remained progressive, but now instead of finding "truth" and the destiny of America by way of a mixture of theology, the literary style of the Bible, and history as the Puritans did, or by way of the Romantic-inspired literary form of Patricians, these new professionals looked to the natural sciences, specifically Darwin's theory of evolution, as a way to explain why America's identity and destiny were a special package. By applying evolutionary laws to the history of America, Frederick Jackson Turner, possibly the most influential 20th-century historian, was able to justify westward expansion and the symbol of the American rugged individual:

> [A] social evolutionary process was working to create the American democratic individualist. The unique characteristics of the American people —their rugged individualism, egalitarianism, self-reliance, practicality, and materialistic outlook on life—all resulted from the evolutionary process of adapting to successive frontier environments. (Grob & Billias, 1972, p. 8)

Another group collecting a large amount of currency in the 20th century is the Progressives, who appeared to contradict the consensus historical writings that developed out of Turner's thesis. This group of American historians, many of whom were heavily involved in writing history texts for secondary schools, managed their narratives in terms of American reform, meaning that history had wrought certain evils, be it individual actions or ideas that developed into practices, thus distorting the "original" American purpose and threatening its liberal democratic future. To protect the future, the Progressive historian had to unearth the "lies" of the past by digging out the "true" intentions of either the founding fathers, or, going back even earlier, the first settlers. History became an ideological weapon to preserve what the historian considered the original national identity (Grob & Billias, 1972; Noble, 1965).

The historian then presented to the public evidence of what America "originally" was, expecting everyone to make "intelligent" structural change in American society. Sometimes explicitly, sometimes implicitly, the Progressive historian petitioned Americans to transcend a failing moral and ethical existence brought on by the vagaries of history. The logic: If Americans acted in moral ways inherited from their forebears, moral ways as revealed by the historian, America could be rescued and placed back on the path of a more perfect society, which exists outside of history.

This political act attempts to preserve what is often some vague notion that America has a prescribed calling. In fact, many 20th-century Progressive American historians, including Richard Hofstadter, Charles and Mary Beard, Arthur Schlesinger, Sr., Arthur Schlesinger, Jr., and Edmund Morgan, meticulously analyzed what they identified as persistent social ills frustrating the progress of America's march. They searched for root causes and self-evident solutions. And more often than not, the solution was for Americans to enter into more moral and intelligent democratic political action as taught to them through the process of schooling. They became modern jeremiad writers.

One who has read a history textbook for elementary or high school, or for most undergraduate college courses for that matter, will recognize such historical tales of America, although it is important to point out that one sees much more of the consensus or progressive oriented approach than the radical (Anyon, 1979).

Histories of education more often than not follow these typical philosophical patterns. These historians (e.g., Cremins, 1964; Curti, 1959;

Kliebard, 1987, 1992; Ravitch, 1985, 2000; Spring, 1972, 1989; Tanner, D., 1991; Tanner, L., 1982; Tanner & Tanner, 1980; Tyack, 1974) mostly concentrate, in terms of the beginnings of the institutionalization of mass public education during the late 19th century, on the specifics of the then current educational practices, academic theories, and specific national leaders who supported those practices popular in that time period. In each fiber of American historical thought—and by no means are these as coherent and unified as presented here for purposes of explanation—historians position themselves in a way that has the effect of preserving, or attempting to enact, what they believe the American identity should and can be.

This impulse toward American identity as some progressive or key force in the development of world history, be it secular, sacred, or both, emerged in part from an inherited historical discourse developed by New England Puritan writers. And this impulse, this way of viewing American identity in relation to history, emerges in the public discussion with great intensity each time a sense of crisis develops. The belief is that if such values are taught, even imposed on young students, these students will become "good" citizens, which translates into an act of maneuvering this abstract notion called America back into a more powerful position in world history, not just economically and militarily, but in the sense of America presenting itself as the spirit of the times, the light of the world.

2

Puritan Moral Symbols: Errand into the Wilderness and the Jeremiad Ritual

It was the larger, American vision the Puritans bequeathed to culture. This was their legacy: a system of sacred–secular symbols . . . for a people intent on progress; a set of rituals of anxiety that could at once encourage and control the energies of free enterprise; a rhetorical mission so broad in its implications, and so specifically American in its applications, that it could facilitate the transitions from Puritan to Yankee, and from errand to manifest destiny and the dream. That these transitions effected changes in rhetoric and ritual goes without saying. But the capacity to accommodate change is proof of vitality, no less in symbolic systems than in social systems.　　　　　　　　　　—*Bercovitch (1993, p. 34)*

THEY CAME to the continent of North America in the Great Migration of 1630, not the first immigrants, not the largest in number. As a distinct population, they lasted not much more than a century before dispersing into denominationalism. Unlike the tales told to American school children during the 20th century, the Puritans were not a small band fleeing England in search of religious freedom, nor were they interested in engaging in the politics of liberty. They were not the forefathers of religious tolerance, of which the Constitution speaks. They were not escaping persecution.

When the word *Puritan* appears in school textbooks, the phrase "city upon the hill" is attached close by on the page, but barely registers as students' attention is directed elsewhere. Such impressions of the colonial Puritans as hard, intolerant, and irrational religious zealots pervade the interpretations of the early American period. Not that the colonial Puritans easily elicit other perspectives. The Salem witch trials and the "insane" practices of trying and burning "witches" quickly rise to the surface and color any cultural analysis within school textbooks. Rarely do high school students graduate without the perfunctory reading of Arthur Miller's *The Crucible,* or Nathaniel Hawthorne's *Scarlet Letter.* Each provides an unflattering portrait of the Puritans.

The colonial Puritans are represented as full of gloom and doom, implying that so grim and rigid a people could never represent an American cultural identity. The page is turned, the Puritans forgotten. After all, America is about optimism. America, students are told, is the land of freedom, liberty, and individualism. America possesses an infinite frontier. Colonial Puritans are presented as a passing phenomenon, although in kinder interpretations they are described as voices in the wilderness preparing the path for the true arrival of the America produced by the American Revolution and the "real" forefathers, Thomas Jefferson, George Washington, John Adams, and others who wrote the "real" "American scripture" (Maier, 1997).

Although such an interpretation has found its place in mainstream educational textbooks, it ignores the workings of the symbolic capital created and refined by the Puritans, capital that remained fixed in the American consciousness as well as within implicit assumptions guiding the purposes of American institutions and moral ways. From the colonial Puritan pens and orations flowed a special, even unique, rhetoric, a symbolic mode of expression and interpretation bordering on the poetic and long outlasting any isolated cultural artifact. These symbolic narratives, lodged in the psyches of later generations by family, school literature and histories, church, and state produced the notion of a unified national identity, that of America, and provided certain inhabitants with a sacred/secular meaning and mission—world redemption. The mission was deemed an errand into the wilderness.

The errand was to redeem the world by the light of example. The colonial Puritans would construct a city upon the hill, a mission to comply with a sacred/secular biblical prophecy that history would come to an end and a transcendental, spiritual age would arise. It was an errand filled with hope. However, this corporate mission also was caged within constant anxiety and peril as the hand of God threatened desolation for individual moral transgressions. Indeed, success of the errand was linked to the moral vigilance of the individual, as guided by the typological maps inscribed within the symbolic narratives penned by the Puritan intellectuals/theologians and leaders.

On boarding the *Arbella* for the journey to the New World, Puritan leader John Winthrop wasted no time instructing those huddled on the deck in the moral imperative of living a measured, vigilant existence. Each *curriculum vitae* ("course of life") had a particular, possibly even overwhelming concern: persistent preparation for the conversion experience. The significance of this experience was tied to the belief in predestination, which generated a kind of anxiety. One had the impulse to find out whether he or she was an elect or not. Conversion meant salvation and the gates of heaven would open upon death. However, as the colonial Puritans were literate people raised in the educational movements toward "rational" thought taking place in Europe during the Reformation, conversion was believed to occur through an interaction of faith and reason. One had to prepare through study and prayer, which would result in exacting moral behavior. The actions of the elect were to exemplify visible sainthood, enlightening and compelling Europe's inhabitants to reform according to the colonial Puritan ways.

In what would set the precedent and tone for the kind of American jeremiads that would later follow, Winthrop taught his fellow travelers the significance of the errand. The final words of Winthrop's jeremiad sermon warned of the price of losing God's map, which would keep the errand on the straight path:

> [T]he lord make it like that of New England: for wee must consider that wee shall be as a Citty upon a Hill, the eies of all people are uppon us; soe that if wee shall deale falsely with our god in this worke wee have undertaken and soe cause him to withdrawe his present help from us, wee shall be made a story and a by-word through the world, wee shall open the mouthes of eneimes to speake evill of the wayes of god and all professours for Gods sake; wee shall shame the faces of many of gods worthy servants, and cause theire prayers to be turned into Cursses upon us, till wee be consumed out of the good land whither wee are going. (Winthrop, 1630/ 1958, p. 93)

The operative notion and phrase for the Puritans was that all those listening to Winthrop would function as visible saints in the material world; "form controls matter." Form became the mental constructs of the Puritan will that were given expression through narrative forms, the most powerful being the symbolic phrase "errand into the wilderness."

THE ERRAND

For the Puritans, the corporate purpose was provided in terms of a task demanded by God. The task, as understood by the Puritans, was to face their destiny head on. The task was the errand: "*Errand:* 1. A. A short trip taken to perform a specified task, usually for another. B. The purpose or object of such a trip. 2. A. A mission; an embassy. B. A message that has been entrusted to one" (American Heritage Dictionary of the English Language, 2000).

The symbol of the errand has proved overtime to be resilient and flexible enough to incorporate many different perspectives. No matter what definition one explores, to run the errand was and is a moral imperative, a process that each individual must undertake to preserve its efficacy as a symbol. Part of running the errand was the reduction of life into two moral categories: good and evil. The Puritan notion of good depended on the existence of earthly evil. The mind needed an object from which to develop a sense of how to proceed in a world that each, in his or her innermost feelings, realized was much more ambiguous than official Puritan theology allowed (Perry, 1944). A Puritan had to depend on his or her will. If one became successful in manipulating (exacting his or her will) social and economic success within the parameters established by community tradition, it was an exhibition of God's grace, which meant that the individual was staying true to the errand path as defined in the jeremiad narratives.

In effect, the notion of evil served as a prime motivation in this struggle to succeed. All things, the Puritans believed, were naturally depraved and as such needed a purifying will to impose goodness on them. Simply, evil became the object of purification. Evil became the lowly matter by which the Puritan will would mold goodness. Evil was not to be ignored, eschewed, or even feared. It was opportunity. It was a means by which to focus the tendency to identify and struggle with moral dilemmas. Each dilemma was an occasion for the individual to impose on the world a form, a moral structure, carved out of the symbolic narrative of the "errand into the wilderness."

As a play off its etymology, it is reasonable to suggest certain paths the errand symbolism could travel. First, although there is no specific or hierarchical order of interpretation here, the errand indicates the act of delivering God's living word, understood here as the moral forms of Calvinism. The colonial Puritan believed that such deliverance would be so powerful it would reform the world. In this sense, the errand was being run for another purpose: Puritans were messengers, harbingers of things to come. Specifically, the Puritans, as a group that ascended in Europe after the Reformation, accepted the notion that the individual had the right and responsibility to interpret that Bible for himself or herself. Such an exercise had the effect, despite great efforts by Protestant leaders in Europe and later colonial Puritan leaders, of providing guidance about how to read the Bible for the *correct* meaning, with the creation of a wide array of words and subsequent symbols. These individual interpretations, because of the nature of symbolic structures and the language from which they arise, all differed in the individual (even internal) space of existence. The need was to externalize these individual understandings and confusing inner experiences. In performing this psychological task, the difference often became more pronounced in the public discussion of meaning. "Confusing inner experiences" means the complex belief, which led to anxiety, that each Puritan was a member of the New Israelites, whose sacred/secular charge was to reform the New World in their image by disseminating their moral forms through prolific writings and institutions. However, it was also realized that they were but earthly beings, cursed with being evil, which would likely ignite God's wrath.

Another interpretative direction is in order. An errand also indicates the possibility of an act run by one's self for one's self. Colonial Puritans believed it was their responsibility to institute an ecclesiastical order, one that would eventually spill back to Europe and give them the power to guide, even control, those elements of secular power throughout Europe. In this sense, the errand functioned as a control operation in terms of imposing on all others the Puritan moral forms and sacred/secular interpretations. Ambiguity and multiplicity of meanings of the errand were important for its preservation. For instance, the errand had a built-in tension: earthly progress in terms of the creation and maintenance of a communal authority, which in turn would fulfill an earthly promise and evoke the end of the world and subsequent spiritual regeneration; and individual salvation. In other words, the errand's success depended on the morality of each individual and how that morality expressed itself in some coherent fashion within the community. Moral vigilance and questioning were not only necessary, but they also would provide the possibility of what was to come: hope and God's grace, or destruction.

Yet, despite many historians' tendency to interpret Puritans as fixating on the sense of doom, as the errand placed a great burden on the individual and the community, it must be remembered that the Puritans' sense of faith, of hope for the future, was attached to the errand from which America would emerge (Bercovitch, 1975, 1978, 1993). To have faith in the errand was to see the world and to understand one's place at that historical juncture as having a destiny. For the Puritans, however, the errand had to have a greater audience. In the most Shakespearean sense, they perceived the world as a stage, and a good theatrical production needed a rapt audience. Europe was to be the New England Puritans' audience, and for the errand to be run in a way that it could succeed, all eyes had to be on them. One of the greatest fears was that Europe would not care, or that it would watch and then grow bored and disinterested, a state of affairs some claim happened.

The errand also served a counterfunction. This symbolic structure allowed for the development of strategies to control radical alternatives that often appear in light of the ideology of individual salvation. This control operation sustained the Puritan notion of community, enabling New England to present itself as an earthly example, as a city upon a hill, for the rest of the world. Over time, the errand would transform into an impulse and discourse of retrieval of something lost, something encrusted with layers of moral distortions, a sinner's mind that had a lapse in memory of mankind's original purpose. The significance of the errand impulse also arises in its tendency to produce a form of eschatological anxiety that operates within the whole nexus of Puritan symbols, imageries, and social realities. They both dreaded and desired a final end to the errand, an immediate conflagration of the world by a God disappointed with or even enraged by mankind's moral transgressions.

Eschatology for the Puritans was both a burdensome and inspirational reference about which they often obsessed. Annihilation meant the end, but it also was a beginning. Only through destruction, made so vivid to the Puritan by the medieval paintings of God's horrific final act of justice, would regeneration of the spirit occur (Miller, 1953, 1957). However, in this theology, multiplicity abounded. Leverenz

(1980) detected a duality in most of the Puritan sermons, indicating the ambiguous and ambivalent nature of the Puritan historical experience:

> Puritan language is most striking in the doubleness of its appeal. It looks both ways: to radical voluntarism, yet to utter submission; to absolute authority, yet limited authority, defined as duties more than power and constrained by mutual obligation from God on down. (p. 7)

At the same time, Puritans constructed themselves as the earthly moral authority, or God's police (Blanke, 1983).

Colonial Puritans possessed a strong sense of self-righteousness. A type of indignation emerged that not only functioned to preserve their heritage in American thought, but also led to disagreements and disruptions within their own ranks. From this tension emerged a vibrant sense of continual moral crisis. This anxiety, this crisis thinking, sustained the errand and gave it force and impetus as something alive and powerful in each American's life. Puritans erected an unattainable ideal that, from their perspective, could only be corrected by God's moral judgment. Bercovitch (1993) identified this gap between fact and ideal as a grave source of anxiety and motivation for the creators of the great American myth of errand and progress:

> The Puritans' vision fed on the distance between fact and promise. Anxiety became their chief means of establishing control. The errand, after all, was by definition a state of unfulfillment, and only a sense of crisis, properly directed and controlled, could guarantee the outcome. (p. 34)

Despite all the social shifts, despite the dispersal of any particular group that can be identified as Puritan, what survived was a sense of moral burden in which each individual carried the weight of the errand on his or her shoulder:

> After his [John Winthrop] death the colony did use its independence to become more and more provincial, more and more tribal . . . but the broader vision that Winthrop stood for could never be wholly subdued. No Puritan could be a Puritan and remain untouched by it, for it arose out of the central Puritan dilemma, the problem of doing right in a world that does wrong. (Morgan, 1958, p. 203)

Because Puritans perceived themselves as earthly exemplars of light, they tended to extend a sense of crisis into all areas and all interactions with others. Any time it was believed the errand was eroding, the Puritans, and those who would later embody the Puritan moral imperative and impulse (the Anglo-Protestant urban middle class of the late 1800s and early 1900s) would enter into what Bercovitch (1993) termed a "ritual of consensus" (p. 29). This means that in American history, Puritans have supplied the symbolic structure and means of interpreting the symbols, within which are set specific habits of logic, so that the impulse will survive. Puritan symbols enabled a wide array of diverse communities to exist together within a geographical space and to claim a piece of the ideal as their own.

Any time this abstract idea began to lose its conventional form and the symbolic web of possible meanings unraveled in a way that threatened the errand, a ritual was entered into that sought to sustain for all the errand into the wilderness. However, an implied caveat was attached: All were welcome as long as each group remained within the boundaries determined by the meaning of the errand itself. Consensus was not about particulars but about transcendence, about how a group experienced embodying the errand. The consensus is what one could call the poetic, possibly impulsive, act of remembering, retrieving, and continuing the errand. The effect of this ritual, one of interpreting and discussing all its possible meanings and effects, was the preservation of the American symbol of the errand into the wilderness as viable and productive. For the colonial Puritans, moral contemplation and consideration (even fixation) were necessary due to the lack of certainty, the all-encompassing ambiguity that was life. The Puritans believed in the production of symbols and the persistent interpretation of those linguistic creations and traditions in an ever-anxious ritual of revealing a map by which to proceed.

The tendency to view the world in the value terms of good and evil as the Puritans did, yet with the recognition of the difficulty of making such a judgment, the impulse toward moral contemplation yielded a harvest of interesting and historically influential tendencies toward expressions of crisis.

THE WILDERNESS

True to the inherent ambiguity of the English language, the term *wilderness* walks in two directions at once. Each meaning saturates the other, despite any attempt to exclude one and privilege the other, which is the usual binary operation of rational thought.

Wilderness was not only the geographical landscape of the continent itself, on which the Puritans assumed they could conform to their rhetorical narratives. The wilderness also symbolized the landscape of the soul, that "heart of darkness" or core of depravity concealed within each person and prepared to betray even the morally steadfast. This wilderness was also perceived as a black void, a nothingness that had to be given form or all would be consumed and destroyed. The void could be given the form of evil or good, dependent on one's moral intentions. The correct moral thoughts could arrive at the right moral action and change the terrain of the world—in both a literal and figural sense.

The void produced only evil unless each individual could generate the forms of moral thought that had the effect of bringing light and goodness to the world. Again, a dark void was not just the external metaphor for the wilderness of America but also for the internal condition of "man." To carry through with that sense of darkness or void, the metaphor also extended to the literal American landscape, waiting in its emptiness, without form, for the Puritans to exert control and shape it into a "city upon the hill" (Heimert, 1953).

This internal and external darkness was a glowing example of how the Puritans operated within the binary oppositions located within the larger notions of good and evil. On one end of the binary register was "light." The metaphor of light weighed heavily in Puritan jeremiads. In part, this is another example of the Puritan moral system, which employed similes as a show of "their hunger for a comprehensive pattern" (Leverenz, 1980, p. 5). For Cotton Mather, the metaphor of light not only signified the lighting of one's own inner sanctum, one's own house so to speak, but also of giving sight to others, to enlighten others by the Puritan example (Blanke, 1983, p. 217). When Puritan Uriah Oakes, president of Harvard College, gave a sermon in 1673 about the Puritan mission, his metaphor of light evoked particular images and emotions from the audience:

> As a City upon a hill ... you have to a considerable Degree enlightened the world as to the pattern of God's House. . . . This our Commonwealth seems to exhibit a little model of the Kingdom of Christ upon Earth. . . . This work of God went on foot and advanced to a good Degree here, (will be) spread over the face of the Earth, and perfected to a greater Degree of

Light. . . . You have been as a Candle in the candlestick that giveth light to
the whole House. (pp. 21–23)

Only after the Puritans' arrival on the shores of the New World did the
American emptiness begin to receive content and greater elaboration
and "enlightenment," not only in the building of villages but also in the
symbolic writings pouring out of New England. The wilderness, representing evil and darkness, was opportunity. In some ways, the Puritans
desired a more tangled and complicated wilderness, for such a state of
existence was challenging. Morality then could be used to analyze and
fixate on a disturbing problem, something not yet certain and in need of
constant written interpretation and public and private elaboration.

Morgan (1944) wrote of one particular Puritan, Michael Wigglesworth, as representative of this tendency to analyze and write daily about
one's pilgrimage through novel moral dilemmas that inevitably arose as
one came in contact with the content of the wilderness. "In this trying
situation Wigglesworth did what any good Puritan would have done;
he prayed and then wrote letters" (p. 43), keeping everyone updated on
his progress. The general Puritan sense, as indicated by the jeremiads,
was that although the wilderness (in all possible meanings) could be
remade, the darkness would return with a persistence that no Puritan
could fight off. The tension was between what the colonial Puritans considered light, those forms that they desired to inscribe on or cull from
the wilderness, and what was dark and evil, the internal and external
threat of void. Each Puritan was to make sense of this tension, to choose
between irreconcilable either/or propositions that the Puritan form of
moral thought produced.

One must either affirm this recurring series of fear and trembling
and redemption in terms of accepting the paradox of the charge and the
reality of mundane life, or collapse into the void; one must find purpose
and meaning in the tension.

PURITAN: PERPETUATING AND COPING
WITH THE JEREMIAD

Apparently, without warning or prior clues, Puritan leaders would sense
that the center was slipping away. They would decry a lack of vigilance
on the part of their flock, a kind of backsliding that placed their/Amer-

ica's cultural identity, and therefore the purpose of the errand, in a precarious position. However, such crucial points in Puritan history also had an interesting effect. Times of crisis served as opportunities for each Puritan to take stock and, in effect, strengthen his or her resolve to stay the moral course laid out by the symbols of the errand. The situation at hand was either good or evil—ambiguity was not an option, although it was an accepted condition of life. Decisions had to be made.

During the 1740s, a century after the arrival of the first Puritan ship, many Puritan preachers rang the moral alarm. Too many of the flock had lost the internal zeal, that condition of piety, and had fallen too much into the other Puritan form of thought: reason. The balance struck by the first American Puritans had been discarded (Greven, 1977). Puritans had always sought methods toward morality, reasoned approaches toward certain behavior. However, it was up to each individual to develop the method through prayer, contemplation, and Biblical interpretation, as long as one eye carefully attended to the moral conventions of the day.

In some ways, Puritans had become victims of their own cultural success. Economic and social success, along with ever fewer numbers of Puritans undergoing, or feeling the need to undergo, conversion experiences, had the effect of a cultural complacency. The cultural mission was being lost. Too many of their brethren, it was believed, had joined in the earthly fray and had forgotten about the greater vision. In fact, this crisis did not emerge out of the loss of living standards or economic fears, but instead out of the sense that many Puritans had become too interested in "easing" the suffering in their lives, and that they were too wrapped up in material luxuries and genteel social conditions (Greven, 1977).

From this anxiety emerged the Great Awakening and the ringing words of Puritan minister Jonathan Edwards, an intellectual, theologian, and Enlightenment thinker. The sense of crisis propelled Edwards to set aside his quiet, intellectual life and his involvement with the works of the Enlightenment, which tended to temper the harsher aspects of Calvinism without erasing the moral impulse or the secular economic activities. He turned away from the Puritan hallmark education, which produced an individual who balanced "rational" thought with passion and mystery, and emphasized pure passion and faith in his sermons to his flock. Edwards perceived the general populace as giving over to a passive state of understanding, a state concerned less with identifying and struggling against evil than with living a comfortable life without suffering.

Edwards condemned those who had dismissed or forgotten the errand into the wilderness. In other words, in order to seek a return to the balance, he attempted to counter the extremes of "reason" with the extremes of passion.

However, Edwards or any fervent Puritan shared the same teleology, the shared Puritan dilemma—doing right in a world that does wrong so that the end may arrive and the spirit be rejuvenated (Miller, 1953, 1957). Whereas medieval paintings provided visible renditions of the end of the world and God's final judgment, Edwards, through words, generated images of all the possible terrors to come if his fellow errand runners continued to engage in moral transgressions. In *Sinners in the Hands of an Angry God*, written during the time of the Great Awakening, Edwards (1740/1999) preached of the ever-looming threat of destruction made necessary by the existence of evil, a destruction that no amount of rational solutions or control over the state of nature could arrest:

> The expression I have chosen from my text, *Their foot shall slide in due time*, seems to imply the following things. . . . 1. That they were always exposed to destruction; as one that stands or walks in slippery places is always exposed to fall. . . . 2. It implies, that they were always exposed to sudden unexpected destruction. As he that walks in slippery places is every moment liable to fall. . . . There is no want of power in God to cast wicked men into hell at any moment. (pp. 65–66)

FROM JEREMIAH TO JEREMIADS

The term *jeremiad* is rooted in the Bible. Specifically, jeremiad, as a form of written or spoken dialogue, originates with the most effusive of prophets, Jeremiah. His is the longest and most poetic book in the Bible (von Rad, 1967).

Jeremiah's link to the Puritans lay not only in his form of communication but also in the seemingly paradoxical content of his writings, which might be summed up in the words "eschatological salvation" (von Rad, 1967, p. 181). What was before must come to an end so that God's planned salvation can progress and eventually occur at some future date. The Puritans took this to heart and took it upon themselves, as the chosen ones, to enact this eschatological salvation. A brief sketch of Jeremiah's style and content of prophecy can supply some insight into the Puritans' sense of election, as well as why the jeremiad suited their temperament so well. Jeremiah, unlike earlier prophets in the Bible, rarely delivered a message from God in a terse, declarative manner. In Jeremiah, one finds that the line between message and messenger is erased. Von Rad, a professor of theology at Heidelberg University and author of what is considered the seminal text on the prophets, wrote of Jeremiah:

> Jeremiah makes much freer use of divine words spoken in the first person; he makes Yahweh launch forth into long complaints, and in other places he raises his own voice to utter complaints. We meet in Jeremiah—perhaps for the first time—with what we today should describe as lyric poetry. (1967, p. 162)

Due to this style of prophecy, Jeremiah did not provide his audience with what would be considered a self-evident "objective" message. Instead, Jeremiah employed graphic symbolism to get God's message across, which was usually a long and painful lament over Jerusalem's rejection of God's anointment. Often the meaning of the message was within the lamentation without any real reference to what could be done to solve the problem. In other words, Jeremiah often transformed God into a complainer. However, Jeremiah also spoke of the future and of hope that a new covenant, a second Jerusalem, would arise. Von Rad (1967) wrote:

> Yet, even although Jeremiah realized that Jerusalem was apparently to be finally rejected, this did not prevent him from ... speaking as if there were still hope, as if it were still possible for the nation to be reached, as though there could still be a decision "before it grows dark, before your feet stumble on the twilight mountains, while you hope for light; but he turns it into gloom." (p. 168; Jer. 13:16)

This tension between what likely will be and what is hoped for is persistent in all of Jeremiah's musings, a tension that colonial Puritans embodied and continually contemplated. That is why Jeremiah placed so much emphasis on salvation as achieved by destroying the conditions that inhibited his people from engaging in "true" moral activity. Jeremiah was not necessarily calling for the people to return to a life that was lived before. In fact, he said that is impossible because once a covenant is broken, it cannot be mended. Instead, the old morality must be made

new again, in a different Jerusalem, in a different time. For Jeremiah, as
for the colonial Puritans, the concern and question was how to do right
in a world that has fallen into iniquity. And in the answer was the continual hope of spiritual rejuvenation. However, Jeremiah often lapsed
into a feared, even certain, inevitability of the abyss that swallows souls
and precludes the spirit from progressing toward its intended end and
new beginning.

In fact, Jeremiah spent much writing in a conversation with God,
which is unusual for a prophet, and confessed of an internal darkness
within himself that did not allow escape into the light provided by
God. However, Jeremiah acknowledged that his office demanded that
he engage in just such impossibility. Part of this internal darkness of
which Jeremiah spoke is the intense need not just to accept God's will,
but also to question and understand the orders. Jeremiah, in spite of
himself, was an intellectual and his complex thought subjected him to a
life of tension between his role as a prophet and his role as a man caught
in the concrete moment, a thinker concerned with the theological problems of the day (von Rad, 1967).

In Jeremiah, one can cautiously begin to grasp the paradoxical life
and powerful symbolism and tension-filled writings of many of the New
England Puritans. The Puritans appropriated Jeremiah's expressive form
—the warnings, the inevitabilities, a sense of appointment and of hope,
the central thesis of eschatological salvation, the continual dialogue with
God and the intellectual and spiritual doubt that comes from questioning. However, they also believed his prophecy applied to them as the
people chosen to engage in a new covenant to build a New Jerusalem.
Such a burden translated into the wedding of secular and ecclesiastical
authority and laws.

For the Puritans, the process of writing a jeremiad served several
functions. In one sense it was a ritual, a thematic reminder to each individual, and to the community at large, that moral action was the root of
earthly existence. As such, it helped the colonial Puritan narrow his or
her focus to the immediate concerns of finding the correct moral action
that best served the sacred/secular purpose. The linguistic structure of
the jeremiad produced a particular effect. Puritans were reduced to
either/or thinking that separated the human condition and the problems that emerged from such a state into categories believed identifiable
and solvable. However, this does not mean the Puritans tended to over-
simplify the notion of morality. Again and again Puritans would, after

making a moral judgment, anguish over and pray about and discuss and question it, despite their confidence that the judgment was the correct one (Bercovitch, 1993; Greven, 1977; Morgan, 1944). Certainty was never experienced as something to delight in, but rather an ideal that God expected all to struggle to achieve.

However, the jeremiad made two cuts simultaneously. In one sense, it cut a mark of optimism in which the individual and the communal identity were connected to particular symbols. This process of connecting meant the individual embodied the words employed to express symbolic meanings, in effect producing a transcendent individual able to function among other transcendent individuals. When these individuals collected into a unified group, a culture emerged that surpassed the earthly and entered into the sacred. Through this act of transcendence, the Puritan identity was translated into a broader American identity, one that provided each individual with the knowledge of himself or herself as embodying the whole and vice versa. By knowledge I mean the understanding that this individual-to-group-to-individual transformation was a badge for each of God's elect to wear. Out of this process would arise a "city upon the hill," an event that would sanction the end of history. America was to be that city. For Puritans, to be God's elect and to run God's errand provided both spiritual and earthly opportunity and reward.

But there was another cut, and this slice revealed an underlying tension. One was likely to fail in such a "city building" undertaking in light of the persistent linguistic ambiguity in the charge. Every time one exacted another cut to interpret and clarify the task, another blade was revealed. The incision exposed the tension between the individual and the community. This tension emerged from the Puritan intellectual tradition generated by the Protestant Reformation. Those involved in the Biblical aspects of the Reformation privileged individual questioning and interpretation of the Bible (Greven, 1977), which had the effect of triggering an antinomy. A Puritan could justify by rational thought either course of action as correctly following the moral imperative. Obey the Puritan ecclesiastical office as cultural authority that knew what was best for the preservation of the errand, or, pursue the intellectual tradition of individual interpretation and moral questioning.

Simultaneous certainty and doubt produced an ambiguity in Puritan existence that had a Jeremiah type of effect. The Puritans found themselves intensely interested in questioning, clarifying, and expressing their intentions and doubts about the correct moral action. Each Puritan was certain about the process of transcendence and cultural identity, and about the universal connections between God, self, community, and the nation. However, she or he recognized that such an identity was tenuous and always exposed to corruption in meaning and purpose. In effect, such an identity had to be protected at all cost, for to lose it was to fail in an errand that the very jeremiad tradition sensed was to fail anyway.

The colonial Puritan identity revolved around the success or failure of the errand, the symbolic construction that served as identity and corporate purpose. In the tradition of Jeremiah, Puritans invested much sacred and secular capital into symbolic constructions as a way of addressing moral earthly and heavenly activity. Even as they wrote and wrote again to clarify moral action, they did so in a more poetic way that rendered precise meaning quite difficult and prevented any over-determination. However, at the same time, this poetic form gave each Puritan a powerful fund of meaning and purpose to push him or her forward toward eschatological salvation (Bercovitch, 1975, 1978; Brumm, 1970). The jeremiad was not just a loud and verbose or poetic complaint the Puritans employed after the first couple of generations in America failed to live up to the chosen status. It was also a celebration of the activity of God's charge that, as Jeremiah understood, humans must attempt to escape the internal darkness that precludes them from God's light and the final end to history.

The jeremiad was a reminder of the great opportunity that, in their minds, was theirs, that was New England's, and that extended to all of America. Miller (1957) identified this irony in the Puritan jeremiads:

> If you read them all through, the total effect, curiously enough, is not at all depressing: you come to the paradoxical realization that they do not bespeak a despairing frame of mind. There is something of a·ritualistic incantation about them: whatever they may signify in realm of theology, in that of psychology they are purgation of the soul; they do not discourage, but actually encourage the community to persist in its heinous conduct. The exhortation to a reformation which never materializes serves as a token payment upon the obligation, and so liberates the debtors. . . . Hence, I suggest that under the guise of this mounting wail of sinfulness . . . the Puritan launched themselves upon the process of Americanization. (pp. 8–9)

Hence, what emerged was an almost schizophrenic sense of the jeremiad process, of that ritual enacted by those reminding others what it means to be an American. One wails over the errand, the task being disregarded or forgotten. But in the next breath comes the smiling celebration over the greatness and importance of the errand, followed by the ironic sense that all the sins and backslidings of society, although lamentable and bad, can still be redeemed in the future.

The jeremiad is a recognition of the paradoxical condition of life, a way of acknowledging without yet paying the debt incurred by the past, while at the same time helping to control how the present is viewed and acted upon (Bercovitch, 1975, 1978; Miller, 1953, 1957). In other words, the errand is still not run. The errand is always in danger, yet it is always the only hope of salvation. The symbolic function of the errand emerged as the one great legacy of the early Puritan culture, a legacy that would supply the consensual basis for all the seemingly different moral discourses struggling over the future of America. In effect, the discourse of the jeremiads used to express the impulse of the errand settled the boundaries of discussion when it came to defining an American identity. The errand rhetoric acted as the dialectical force between those discourses celebrating the current American cultural conditions, which were considered authentic, and those dissenting and claiming Americans were not staying true to their errand. The errand rhetoric afforded a control operation to sustain what became this abstract notion of America as something more than just the physical and political/geographical boundaries of the United States. America was simply accepted, by the Colonials and by the majority of Americans to this day, as the last, best hope of Western civilization. Writer after writer set out with the same passionate assumption, even those that penned protests against what America had become in their eyes, or better, what America had lost during its history (Bercovitch, 1993): America had, and still has, an errand into the wilderness. This phrase had, and continues to have, a psychological hold on the American imagination as well as on the logic with which we approach our institutions. The jeremiad, while finding a specific place within the religious sermon, constituted a narrative logic that permeated and acted as a foundation for other communal institutions.

This Puritan intellectual tradition of moral questioning in part led to devising a series of institutions, each with their educational element: family, school, government, and finally church. Each institution worked in conjunction with the others to sustain Puritan culture and identity as represented by the symbol of the errand into the wilderness. Examining Puritan forms of education, the search for one's calling, as a means of creating what Kaufmann (1999) labeled "institutional individualism," provides some groundwork for understanding how the moral imperative generated a perception in the late 1800s that mass public education was necessary to preserve America's grand purpose.

3

Finding Order and Balance
Between Faith and Reason
Through Educational Maps

The theorists of New England thought of society as a unit . . . as an organism . . . with all parts subordinate to the whole, all members contributing a definite share, every person occupying a particular status. . . . Puritans did not think that the state was merely an umpire, standing on the sidelines of a contest. . . . The state to them was an active instrument of leadership, discipline, and, wherever necessary, of coercion; it legislated over any or all aspects of human behavior, it not merely regulated misconduct but undertook to inspire and direct all conduct.   —*Perry (1944, p. 143)*

ONCE COLONIAL Puritans stopped seeking Europe's attention and turned their gaze to the continent on which they stood, they wanted nothing less than to rule America in all of its forms and steer it toward a sacred/secular destiny (Bercovitch, 1975, 1978). Such high expectations and psychological impulses toward transcendent purposes could not be had by faith and pietism alone. Humane knowledge could and should not be avoided as it provided a "reasoned method" by which to map out and then explicate not just an individual life moving toward spiritual conversion, but a nation leading the world toward redemption. For Puritans, each individual's "course in life"—a literal translation of John Calvin's phrase *curriculum vitae*—was to reflect the historical course of America as a corporate nation (Bercovitch, 1978; Emerson, 1977; Kaufmann, 1999).

A reasoned method entailed an ordering, enumerating, and explaining of experiences, each building on the other until a narrative map of spiritual completion was outlined. For the individual, this was nothing less than inscribing a spiritual autobiography. The ability to produce this map indicated training in what Puritans accepted as a method of reason. This method and intellectual and spiritual trajectory reproduced and was reproduced by the institutions of family, school, church, and civil life, all in the effort to strike a balance between revelation of faith and human knowledge. Whereas faith elided the revelatory nature of the ultimate mystery, the physical world was a function of reason. According to Puritan theologians/civil leaders, God was the source of reason. And reason articulated itself in world creation. Each colonial Puritan child was inculcated from birth in this logic. Hence, it made sense to ascertain God's will in the world by way of a reasoned method (Emerson, 1977; Miller, 1957; Morgan, 1988). These cultural traits, brought over from Europe, summarized the means and functions of education.

Such purposes of education have gone mostly unexcavated, despite being implemented not only in each township but also at the first American university, Harvard University, which was to become the basic model of education throughout the centuries (Miller, 1953; Morison, 1936). Even as the Latin Grammar School transformed in the 1800s into the Common School, which dictated a shift in subject matter emphasis, the typical means by which the rhetorical, curricular, and pedagogical characteristics of "teaching" and "learning" would be structured and transmitted was thoroughly rooted. This system of constituting and delivering knowledge was connected to the colonial Puritans appropriation of the rhetorical, curricular, and pedagogical processes of Peter Ramus, the 16th-century European arts master. Ramus developed a rhetorical method of dialectic that became the basis of his pedagogy as well as the first modern linear curriculum map to simplify the order and transmission of knowledge. The intent was to develop a method to control the flow and interpretation of predescribed knowledge by which to inculcate each child and adult.

But this pedagogical method went beyond classroom instruction to transmit cultural knowledge. According to Ramus, the students were to appropriate his rhetorical lens, his reasoned method, which involved taking one's solitary mental thoughts and making them "plain" to another. The student was to take this classroom lens and apply it to the entire world, which is evident in the development of jeremiads. As discussed in the previous chapter, jeremiads functioned from the same rhetorical pattern and assumptions in constructing the world. Ramus refined a method through which the student would use a linear logic to order and map out the world—externally and internally—so that uncertainty would be erased. Of course, the interest in this notion of education by the colonial Puritans spoke to their intense desire to create maps for individuals to live the kind of life that would support the greater institutional bodies and their national mission (Kaufmann, 1999). Simply, the activity produced through the acceptance of "method" as the means to guide and plot one's future and the nation's future, and as the means to perpetuate particular agendas on the meaning and value of American identity, gradually became nothing less than "natural," an unquestioned assumption.

Crucial to the success of the Puritans' construction of a symbolic narrative, which reflected the rhetorical trajectory delivered through a reasoned method, was how the Puritans perceived the nature of the "individual" and the "institutional."

CALL TOWARD INSTITUTIONAL INDIVIDUALISM

Although the state actively participated in the lives of citizens, for most Puritans, the errand symbols diverted their interpretations of the moral function of the ecclesiastical order away from any notion that the individual was being oppressed. For most Puritans, there existed something more than the material world, more than the individual, something that was represented by the ecclesiastical authority. The individual expression became representative of the community, an embodied statement of the community and its tradition of transcending both individual and group. Joining a community was an act of freedom to choose to become an "individual." For New England Congregationalists, the notion of *individual* was mutually dependent on the existence of the notion of *institution*. The etymology of *individual* begins with the Latin root *dividere*, meaning to divide, and prefaced by *in-*, translated as "not," giving us the term individual as meaning "not dividable," or "indivisible," which strikes the modern sensibility as strange. Williams (1983) explained that the term *individual* is usually perceived as something separate from, whereas "indivisible" is something connected to, something else.

Before the 17th century, the dominant meaning of the term individual indicated something or someone that could not be separated or distinguished from the group. To be an individual, in the modern sense of the word, would have meant one who was eccentric, incomprehensible, and who refused to participate in the "common sense." However, Kaufmann (1999) pointed out how the word came to mean the opposite:

> By the . . . nineteenth century (i.e. rugged, self-reliant, Emersonian individualism), the dominant meaning of individual came closer to how we now think of the word: something or someone that is unique, special, distinguishable from commonalties. This individual too is indivisible— but only from himself or herself; he or she can be divided from the group but cannot be further divided. Modern individuality is the irreducible unit of identity. (p. 18)

In effect, the 17th-century individual would identify himself or herself in terms of how he or she resembled others, whereas the modern individual derives a sense of self from how he or she is different from others within shared cultural institutions. New England Puritans demonstrated the relational sense of individual most obviously in America. For the colonial Puritans, an individual was not perceived as a discrete entity struck deaf and then told to listen for his or her calling. The Puritan system provided a heavily patriarchal constraint system that gave contour and voice to one's possible identities (Kaufmann, 1999). The cultural paradigm worked in this way. The Puritan network of institutions was patterned from the filial arrangement, for a child generally made his or her acquaintance with the world through family. Puritans inherited an English patriarchal system and a theological system within which the absolute Other was the ultimate male authority figure. The father was responsible for these relations (Stone, 1979).

However, it was recognized that the child had to move beyond the immediate family and enter into social and spiritual affiliations. The impetus for this cultural trajectory was basic human desire, which for the Puritans was a factual state of existence, neither good nor bad but neutral. Puritans firmly believed that individuals possessed some natural desire to relate with a paternal ideal, with the ultimate affiliation being the absolute Other.

According to this social construct, a child would begin by idealizing the immediate father, but would then soon recognize weaknesses or moral cracks and seek a better father and embody his traits. Each institution communicated to a young Puritan some symbolic leader who was to represent the more ideal father. The child was to be "naturally" drawn to imitation, with each successive paternal figure presenting a more pure ideal, until the child finally experienced a conversion to the "original" father, the absolute Other. Only then, in this spiritual relation, did one become an individual. These paternal relations guided one's *curriculum vitae*. From the historical evidence available, for the most part, Puritan male and females did not perceive such analogies and institutional structures as oppressive.

In fact, the first filial arrangement was the only institution to which one did not voluntarily submit (Greven, 1977; Kaufmann, 1999). Through interaction with the family, in terms of direct and indirect instruction, the child embodied the filial cultural arrangement that shaped one's identity. However, by the age of 14, a child began acting on the impulse toward affiliation by rejecting the immediate family in favor of more ideal affiliations. The boy or girl would often turn his or her attention and behavior to other institutions, such as school and scholarly study if he decided to become a clergyman, or to an apprenticeship if he or she wanted to become a craftsman or handmaiden or seamstress. An apprenticeship would last up to 7 years. Once a decision was made, rarely could one turn back (Morgan, 1944).

As a Puritan moved from one institutional sphere of existence to the next, he or she experienced a shift from filial to affiliate relations. In this process, a Puritan was perceived as rejecting the previous arrangement in a cultural desire to find a more ideal relation with a paternal other.

Significant for the individual, then, was not to discern differences between himself or herself and another being, but instead to identify and appropriate the differences between cultural institutions, each one promising a different paternal appeal (Kaufmann, 1999). After this decision, the individual affiliated with the community at large, which later developed into an affiliation with a national identity—an American—and then the congregation at church, or, more accurately, the minister himself as the next ideal father. Finally, in the act of *Christi imitatio*, one became a complete individual and chose willingly to submit to and identify with the absolute Other. Although this took years of study and interior analysis, Puritans actually perceived this as a motion back in time to reunite with the original ideal father.

In the network of these linear, chronological, and method-oriented affiliations, the individual was not expected to eradicate all differences and only resemble one's immediate family. To deviate was the human soul's "natural" state, for it no longer dwelled as one with the absolute Other. However, this deviation was connected to sin, and sin took on forms unique to each individual. Puritans desired to return to a moment without sin that, in a true Puritan paradox, was never fully possible while living on earth. To return to some original condition was to have the effect of wiping away all differences, all sin, and experiencing God as no longer other, but one and the same as the individual. The only differences expected to survive in the individual were the differences between institutions, as well as those practices that distinguished Puritans from Catholics or other denominations that were not Congregationalist.

Although this process strikes the modern sensibility as an act of submission (anathema to one's personal freedom of expression), to the colonial Puritans it was instead an act of volition. A choice to surrender to something beyond one's self was freely made, demonstrating a strong "devotion to the purest institutional authorities. . . . Following the logic of affiliation, to strengthen these institutions was also to strengthen, not diminish one's sense of self. . . . To exist without an institutional affiliation was to be abandoned to one's corrupt and degenerate self" (Kaufmann, 1999, p. 3).

However, the responsibilities and obligations did not flow one way. If the institutional leaders failed to elevate their actions to communal standards, specifically in terms of visible sainthood, Puritan congregations revoked all power. The institution, meaning those leaders who represented the sacredness of each institution, had to adhere to the paternal ideal of guiding and serving the collection of individuals to justify each individual's willingness to embody institutional identity (Kaufmann, 1999; Stone, 1979). Simply put, a father had to take care of and guide his flock. The mother was to protect the child and support the father's leadership.

What is significant is that a cultural framework existed to help one develop a "lens," to use an anthropological term. An individual would assume this lens to determine his or her life task, perceived as one's natural place within society, through a search of the interior and exterior known and unknown. From this perspective, the institutional structure of Puritan society was not set up to oppress one's free will, but actually made one's individuality and identity possible. Without it, no spiritual or mundane life had any meaning, for it was believed that the person could not transcend his or her condition without a social form or language of interpretation and institutional guidance.

Only when possessive individualism emerged with capitalism as a privileged social form were institutions considered hindrances to the individual's desire for "personal expression" or "freedom." Mass school movements of the late 1800s and early 1900s embraced and institutionalized these assumptions of what it meant to be an individual and the rhetorical methods to control and direct the individual. In effect, the later bureaucratic structure of public schools adopted an understanding of curriculum that treated the individual as an economic resource, a piece of raw material to be molded into a refined product (Kliebard, 1987, 1992). However, before the advent of mass public schooling, the notion of the calling, while circumscribed by the conditions of a patriarchal society, did generate much educational literature aimed toward providing the individual with a sacred/secular curriculum map of personal and, therefore, national salvation.

PURITAN CALL: INTERIOR SEARCH AND ARCHETYPAL GUIDES

In a discussion of Puritan leader John Winthrop's duties as a social ruler and visible saint, Bercovitch (1975) interpreted the significance of the two-fold concept of calling—the inward call to redemption and the summons to a social vocation imposed on man by God for the Common Good:

> In keeping with their militant worldliness, the Puritans laid special emphasis on vocation. . . . Invoking various scriptural models, they distinguished the merely good ruler from the saintly ruler, and insisted that the saintly ruler reflect his inward calling in his social role. . . . As his vocation was a summons from god, so his belief led him to do well in public office. (p. 6)

This concept of the calling, then, placed demands not only on the social institutions to care for and watch over the individual, but also on the individual to serve the Puritan institutions as a visible saint, no matter the vocation. However, service was not possible unless one was attentive to a particular voice. One listened for the call of the absolute Other. This listener strained to catch the summons, which was most audible when one was deep in study or reflecting on and praying for guidance through the internal wilderness of the soul.

For the colonial Puritans, though, the soul had lost its original identity. After the Biblical fall of Adam and Eve, the dwelling no longer was a transparent pool reflecting God's light, but an overgrown and opaque wasteland that had to be eradicated and given order through institutional individualism and purpose through the symbolic narrative of the "errand" and its product, "city upon a hill." As strict Calvinists, these colonials refuted the notion that one could go at this exploration of, or better, campaign against, the interior wilderness without a spiritual sense of method. For any hope of achieving transcendence, one had to have a lens, a language by which to articulate one's findings.

Although it was believed that each individual's inward turn had different tones and textures and dark creatures to be eradicated, the worst being any residue of an unencumbered self, the Puritans brought with them from Europe an empirical, experiential approach to understanding the world and the self. With this paradigm came the assumption that not only could one locate God in the external world through the objective study of nature, but the same would hold true for the inner life of mankind. The individual's interiority was an object subjectively analyzed, studied, and dissected, even though the outcome often could not be articulated in the language of science or reason (Greaves, 1969). Humans needed mediation. According to the colonial Puritans, God provided language as a means to understand and articulate, even though it was an imperfect tool, often as likely to create pitfalls and ambiguous signposts as to explain and clarify. But for the Puritan mind, this was not an undesirable condition.

Language was given to slow humans down, for the journey to the absolute Other needed time for reflection and deep understanding, neither of which could or should happen immediately. According to colonial Puritan belief, if God was experienced too quickly, the individual would be ruined, overloaded with too much before enough maturity of flesh and thought could control the spiritual knowledge. Time and maturation were needed to work through each unique though sinful state, as represented by the metaphor of the wilderness. A linguistic means also was needed to begin to understand what was happening during this internal pilgrimage.

For the colonial Puritans, this was a recursive activity, for one simply did not move from step A to step B of salvation. The individual revisited every doubt, concern, and moral action to think through, pray about, and interpret again the meaning of each situation and how it affected his or her life's course. For the recursive journey of interiority, a particular kind of language, something between science and poetry, appeared to provide a means of mediating the complexity of understanding the experience of "knowing one's self" and giving it articulation. Meaning emerged out of the act of articulating, which was not only a public and necessary activity but also one that entailed an ordering of events that then produced a narrative sacred/secular tale. And this spiritual autobiography followed a narrative, rhetorical form learned in school and from jeremiad sermons and theological/historical writings of leaders.

Cotton Mather penned individual expressions of *curriculum vitae* (spiritual autobiographies, treatises, jeremiads, and biographical books and sermons) intended to map out the stories of those Puritans deemed visible saints. The figures of these stories of individual journeys through the exterior and interior wilderness became archetypes—figural/historical representations of spiritual transcendence. Although the happenings and the individuals were real (thus historical), every action, thought, and temptation each experienced was written in a way that coincided with the trials of Christ or the journey of some other Biblical character also imitating Christ (thus figural). Responding to the call, then, required an interpretive framework to traverse the interior path and to give the desires, temptations, and tribulations symbolic significance. This narrative means of interpreting the interior response to the calling satisfied the empirical sense of reality as well as the spiritual sense of temporality. Each visible saint had to hear the calling, respond to it, enter into a wilderness, fight temptation of sensual existence, and be given grace. Out of the interpretation of cultural texts, one arrived at a destination and, therefore, vocation. This was a cultural means by which to bring individuals into the institutional flock and protect and further the errand into the wilderness.

Cotton Mather performed this ingenious service by developing typologies—moral guide maps of individuals who, over time, became representative American identities. Through the historical rendering of a particular Puritan life, the next generation of Puritans would have a well-inscribed map to follow. One of the most important typologies that Mather developed was that of John Winthrop, the leader of the first generation of New England Puritans.

Mather invested Winthrop with the attributes of Biblical figures: Christ, speaking to the Christological influence on the Puritan theology; and Nehemia, who led his people out of Babylon back to the Promised Land. Mather, in one chapter of his *Magnalia,* entitled "Nehemias Americanus," applied to America, as a symbol, the moral attributes of Winthrop. He charged each American with the moral imperative of embodying these attributes, and his narrative on Winthrop's life became a map by which to do so. If each American succeeded, then America, as symbol and material reality, would be secure. America could keep its ordained position as light of the world and as a sacred/secular earthly Utopia, a city upon the hill, a lofty place that the travails of history could never reach. As Bercovitch (1975) wrote, "[T]he logic of Mather's phrase . . . moves from the personal to the historical (Nehemiah to the New World) and in doing so, links the biblical hero, the New England Magistrate, and the enterprise at large in an emphatically American design" (p. ix).

Before an individual can become a true "individual," he or she must embody the symbolism of the American identity as represented by the interlocking of Winthrop, Christ, redemption, and America. This was not mere hagiography in which the hero was presented in a thoroughly abstract form with no real human qualities. Instead, Mather accepted the basic depravity of his heroes and the need for redemption. Winthrop was no exception. Mather portrayed Winthrop as having to go through many temptations, providing the sense that Winthrop had to overcome numerous character faults early on in his life in order to be redeemed and become the literal/figural saint of the colonial Puritans. In these narratives, the individual did not attempt to escape the darkness of the interior wilderness but instead attempted to cut an opening that would allow the light of the absolute Other to filter in and cleanse the self.

The consequence of a Puritan individual not responding to this call was grave. The individual would succumb to the interior thicket, which would in turn infiltrate the congregational/institutional identity, invite the rule of ignorance, and devastate the Puritan project of creating a "city upon the hill" (Bercovitch, 1975). Winthrop employed the phrase "city upon the hill" not only as a promise of what might happen if colonial Puritans were successful, but also as a warning to reflect the seriousness of each individual's obligation to respond to the call.

This ideology placed a heavy burden on each individual, despite Puritans "fear and loathing" of the idea that any particular self could have priority over or separate from the spiritual project. This was an interesting bind. One had to concentrate, often to the point of obsession, on one's self to make the necessary affiliations and relations to institutions and the absolute Other. This is a significant juxtaposition to another ideology of self-identity that was spreading across Europe, that of the humanist celebration of the self as autonomous and unhindered by history or existing institutions.

Both humanists and Puritans professed interest in the world, but they differed on what kind of emphasis should be placed on the individual. Both worldviews had perceptions that unleashed an intense impulse toward self-study, demonstrated in the resurrection of the old Socratic adage, in a Latin translation of the Greek, *Scito te Ipsum* (know thy self). However, for the humanists, this command had the effect of celebrating the notion of an autonomous, secular self, and the

> primacy of the single separate person, and justifies his self study on its intrinsic merits, without pretense at religious or even moral instruction. He assumes that what he has thought and done will interest others because it is authentically his, the product of his own personality in all its rich uniqueness. The mode of identity he offers posits that no two selves are alike. (Bercovitch, 1975, pp. 11–12)

The Puritans interpreted this command with a different lens. One did not find glory in his or her individual self, only greed and pride and a thicket of sin. The impulse was to analyze and examine one's interiority through the use of cultural texts in order to weed out the iniquitous self and transcend to a spiritual self. During the Renaissance, when mirrors became popularized, many sought within the reflection a glimpse of their true inner selves. However, Puritans looked for just the opposite. The less a Puritan saw himself or herself in the mirror the better. Even better was to cast no reflection at all. A reflection of one's self without the absolute Other shining through, or at least looking over his or her shoulder, was but an image of personal failure.

The interior self blocked true spiritual effervescence because of the interior self's state of darkness and guilt. This was a remarkable dilemma, for the desire to annihilate one's interior self and replace the empty reflection with an image of God actually had the effect of celebrating an obsession with the self. The proliferation of spiritual autobiographies, which became narratives of one's journey toward conversion and were used as a resource, along with diaries and letters, for public testimonials before the congregation, indicates the significance Puritans placed on maintaining a record of one's earthly and spiritual self. The harder one worked to become more Christ-like, the greater was the desire to impose one's self on the world and display visible sainthood. This self work could only occur, though, if one was "educated" in the means by which to inquire into the interior and exterior world. The spiritual narratives required a literate population disposed toward understanding the rhetorical forms that the writings took. Colonial Puritans could read Cotton Mather's work on John Winthrop and make sense of it as an exemplary model because of their educational training in the rhetorical methods and symbolic formations used in transmitting cultural information from generation to generation.

RAMUS MAPS AND COLONIAL PURITAN SCHOOLING

For the New England Puritans, schooling, especially in terms of rudimentary literacy, was a serious, legal requirement. It provided the basic tools not only to answer the interior call but also to become a capable, worldly individual with craft and intelligence to understand the full meaning of world activity. In 1641, John Cotton developed a type of formal education for children that exacted from the father a heavy investment of time and money:

> According to law every father had to see that his children were instructed in some honest lawful calling, labour or employment, either in husbandry, or some other trade profitable for themselves, and the commonwealth if they will not or cannot train them up in learning to fit them for higher employments. (p. 439)

Crucial to the process of revealing one's vocation was the obligation to gain knowledge of the world, for God was in all things and the one able to "read" the text of the world enhanced his or her chances for salvation.

Ignorance of world knowledge, as opposed to truth revealed to an individual by God, threatened one's salvation and the perpetuation of the Puritan errand of creating a city upon the hill.

> Truth which came by ordinary means, as in science, philosophy, and the arts, would not contradict but enhance revealed truth. . . . At best human

erudition was so full of God's truth that its only enemy in Puritan eyes was ignorance; it was so closely related to God as the author of all truth that it tended toward the perfection of the human mind. (Greaves, 1969, p. 121)

Perfection, that quest for visible sainthood, needed a navigational tool, a means to construct the world based on explicating the mental images one produced in the belief that those images were given by God. A particular Renaissance arts master, Peter Ramus, created just such a literal map that was used to generate not only the kind of logic employed in jeremiads, but also the curricula in colonial Puritan schools.

During the 16th century, Ramus developed for university education —although primary and secondary schools quickly adopted his structure—a map that attempted to codify knowledge and present the reader with a linear process by which to attain that knowledge. His textbooks, encyclopedic in form and content in that they were believed to provide information to the student in systematic and efficient ways, spread across Europe and America (Ong, 1971). Just as the printing press standardized the means to spread the content of one's thought throughout Europe, Ramus created ways to standardize the knowledge that would be included in these texts and how those texts should be taught.

Ramus' maps were wildly popular in Calvinist universities throughout Europe. When, in the mid-1600s, the Puritans developed Harvard's course of study, the leaders adopted Ramus' logic and curriculum maps. Puritans subscribed to Ramus' assumptions that nothing was useable in any text or object of study, including one's interior self, unless it was first analyzed. Also, information discerned from the analysis had to have some "utilitarian" function in the world. Knowledge for knowledge's sake was useless to the colonial Puritans, and to Ramus.

Puritans believed the maps proved well suited to rationalize and order the integration of the Christian view of revealed truth and the language and knowledge of the new learning, specifically the scientific and philosophical paradigms arising out of the Renaissance (Doll, 1993). However, in the beginning, Ramist mapping was just part of the colonial Puritan sense of external curriculum. It was much more involved in attempting to strike a balance or to show how the knowledge of science and the knowledge of experiential faith were not in opposition, but that both announced the truth, although in different languages. Scholarship not only led to one becoming a clergyman or civil leader, for these were just a couple of possible vocations. Curriculum also had to prepare the vocations of the "working" world.

This is not to say that the Puritans believed that Ramist logic and the maps that arose from this logic and reason would lead to experiencing God, only that without a reasoned, linear method, one could never understand and explicate, by way of a spiritual narration, one's conversion. In fact, Ramism found cultural sanction not just through the use of Ramus' methods at fledgling Harvard University, but also in its being adopted by New England Puritan preachers and schoolmasters, many of whom came from the Harvard ranks. The colonial Puritan leaders, didactically trained in and by Ramist curriculum maps at British universities before coming to America, eagerly appropriated its utilitarian offerings (Miller, 1953; Morgan, 1988; Ong, 1958, 1971).

Ramism's curricular maps for didactically guiding pedagogy specifically supplied a highly efficient and simplified means of reaching an audience beyond the previously identified, converted elect of each Congregational church. Ramism was, at least for Puritans, primarily a method of explanation to be used by the public at large, and a deep and incessantly acted-upon impulse rooted within the Puritan spirit:

> The adoption of Ramism thus did not mean a yielding to reason, but rather to its specifically utilitarian employment for two different audiences. First, those who were learned but who had not yet been converted could be brought to an "external' (or preparationist) appreciation of the procedures of Christianity; secondly, for those whom faith had already made regenerate, the structures of reason, familiar from secular existence, could be shown to be compatible with the truths of revelation. While Ramism did not overwhelm its opposition in the [English] universities . . . it became extremely popular among those who sought to explain their knowledge to a wider audience. These included Puritan preachers and schoolmasters. (Morgan, 1988, p. 112)

According to Puritan doctrine, one had to become learned in and through the method of reason as described diagrammatically by Ramus and reproduced in the institutions of family, school, church, and civil life so that a balance could be struck between the revelation of faith and humane knowledge (Emerson, 1977; Miller, 1957; Morgan, 1988).

Uncertainty was the bane of Puritan existence, as in the well-reported psychological anxiety produced by the nagging doubt of whether one was to undergo conversion or not. Ramist method provided not only psychological comfort but a "form" by which to place over, understand, and so control the world: "The first Puritans did indeed succeed in impressing upon the *tabula rasa* of America a European and Protestant seal. With their articulated sciences of theology, psychology, logic and rhetoric, they possessed coherent answers to all conceivable contingencies" (Miller, 1953, p. 14).

PURITAN FONDNESS FOR SECULAR LEARNING

Puritans exhibited great devotion to secular learning, especially for those who were inclined toward the professions of schoolmaster and minister (Emerson, 1977; Haller, 1957; Miller, 1953; Morgan, 1988). In fact, the Puritans possessed a predisposition toward secular learning due to their lack of immunity from the larger cultural shifts produced in Europe during the Reformation. Puritans in general grew up in a period of university expansion and took full advantage of it, spending much of their childhood studying the trivium and quadrivium. "As the congregations became more learned, they placed a higher standard of learning on the preacher, who it was assumed should always be intellectually a step ahead of his flock" (Morgan, 1988, p. 95).

This shift toward acknowledging the importance of secular reason for all individuals, especially for those who were to interpret and carry the Bible's word to the masses, produced the first traces of professionalization of those involved in education. The vocations of minister and schoolmaster were symbolically and often literally considered as one and the same. The highest ministerial post in Boston was the rank of Teacher. A Harvard graduate often held both posts in towns outside of Boston. The connection between the clergy and schoolmaster is significant, for if the two posts were not held by the same individual, each was expected to complement the other (Miller, 1953; Morgan, 1988). Clergy and schoolmaster were responsible for instructing others how to interpret not just the Bible, which was primary in all of learning, but all texts of the secular canon. It was not uncommon for clergy to quote from the ancient wisdom of the Greeks or Romans.

To cast about for a secular quote was not only an understandable condition and expression of one's learning, but also an identifiable means by which the clergy sought to explain as "plainly" as possible the correct, commonsense interpretation of the Word. In the mouths of clergy and schoolmaster, the sacred and secular collided. Schoolmasters often used sermons as a form of curricular lesson. Students were directed to take notes during the sermon and practice receiving the same kind of didactic transmission of information that took place in the classroom. This made sense, as the sermon was structured along Ramist logic and delivered by the Ramist didactic in ways similar to the schoolmaster's curriculum and pedagogy. Each valued memorization and the organization of ideas in logical, topical forms that suited memorization (Miller, 1953; Morgan, 1988).

Over time, the ministry began to credential no one as a minister without a university education (Morgan, 1988). Because so many of the rural clergy also became schoolmasters, the mentality of professionalization was easily extended to the teacher. Such secular and religious interdependence made the Puritans friendly toward the notion of logic and method as the most useful tools in life. What may have eventually undermined the religious significance intended by Puritan notions of study was the fact that Puritans believed that God was rational and, therefore, created humankind as rational creatures and He spoke to them in the ways of reason. This emphasis on the rational led to a greater emphasis, in school, being placed on students developing empirical understanding rather than in internal preparation for conversion. As Cotton Mather wrote in *A Man of Reason,* "The Power and Process of Reason is Natural to the Soul of Man" (quoted in Miller, 1953, p. 419). And elsewhere in his treatise, Mather reiterated this notion: "The Voice of Reason, is the Voice of God" (quoted in Miller, 1953, p. 427).

According to Miller (1953):

Ramus held that logic was derived from experience by "invention." Therefore, logic had to remain faithful to reality [nature]: it could not create fanciful constructions, but only make replicas of that pattern of ideas embodied in creation. If God so desired, He could call His saints by an audible voice, or by investing them with a halo visible to the naked eye. Instead, He had chosen to deal with them as with rational creatures. . . . He has provided that the Word should come to men's ears externally and sensibly. (pp. 74–75)

Ramist methodology enabled the schoolmaster and minister to "break down" knowledge in both Bible and textbook and convey it so that pupils could understand the transmissions as self-evident and com-monsensical. As Mages (1999) explained Ramus' approach:

> Employing this Ramean method, one first identified the concept to be investigated then divided it into halves, halved these again in turn, and so on until all the components were established. Once all the reasons or concepts were laid out, then an individual could start combining them to form arguments. (p. 97)

In other words, the belief was that man, due to the Fall, could not receive wisdom directly from God. Therefore, God placed "it [reason] in things, from which it is radiated to the brain through the perceiving senses, as is the smell of flowers through the nostrils" (Miller, 1953, p. 428). The rules of Ramist dialectic enabled the user to apply a logical form to what he or she apprehended, giving it order and transmitting the mental construct to others. Over time Puritans shifted their understanding of reason as an act of ordering a mental perception, and in practice a slight adjustment was made. Reason was no longer a systematic logic applied to the world, but instead an innate ability to see the self-evident truth for oneself. Ramist logic and "plain style" was retained for the pedagog-ical expediency of simplifying, ordering, and transmitting each neces-sary function for innate reason to be communicated.

If God made man's mind a rational mechanism constructed to hear God's whispers, then the individual must, as clearly as possible, articu-late those images, for they are the most "natural" and reflect the true structure of the "natural" world. In others words, one must strive for the "plainest speaking." Plain speaking was the Ramist form within which Puritans put their innate grasp of reason. As Miller (1953) explained, "Although Puritans understood that rhetoric appealed to emotions, they strove by might and man to chain their language to logical propositions, and to penetrate to the affections of auditors only by thrusting an argu-ment through their reasons" (p. 12).

Moreover, the Ramist proposal was that the world must first be marched through his diagrammatic structure so that the listener or the reader would most easily and quickly pick up on what was being said and how to interpret those images. This method employed by minister and schoolmaster was most readily visible, as discussed earlier, in the development of the Puritan jeremiad—that sermon of despair and hope, structured through Ramist logic.

Because of the psychological underpinnings of the Puritans' sense of mission, part and parcel of this frame of mind was the fear that all would be lost, that the wilderness (that which lay in front of them in America and that which existed in every heart) would overcome and destroy their mission unless chaos (wilderness) was turned to order. Order was the deep impulse (Doll, 1993, 1998; Hamilton, 1990). Due to this impulse, the clergy not only developed a means to express the fears, but also provided a dichotomizing method by which to overcome them.

Colonial Puritans possessed an impulse toward explication of one's experiences while trying to prepare for and grasp God's reasoned intentions lodged in all things. This was coupled with a need to identify and eradicate evil. The Ramist method allowed them to do both, as the Ramist logical operations gave Puritans the form by which to decide what was good and what was evil and then explain in great detail this apprehension.

The Ramist dialectical task of breaking down a perception into a dichotomy, then choosing as good the preferred oppositional pole, allowed each Puritan to locate God's reason and wisdom and chart it. This dichotomizing operation was extremely important, especially for the ministers, due to the need to identify evil and spell it out in logical detail to the congregation. The schoolmaster utilized the same operation as well. What is telling is the fact that the clergy handed out Ramist diagrams or maps to help the congregation follow along with the sermon just as the schoolmaster guided students in copying notes (Morgan, 1988). Such diagrams directed one's thinking toward a prescribed path. The intent was not to broaden the consciousness of the congregation and the school children, but to instruct them in a highly delineated understanding of correct knowledge and interpretation, in terms of schoolmasters, and on the correct living and preparation of ministers.

Puritan preachers used Ramism not because it removed blockages to the free use of reason, but rather because it was constructed such that it allowed only one direction for man's reason. Ramus offered a guide to Puritans in an attempt to explain the coordination of human individual struggle with the external universe. For the Puritans, the Ramist method provided certainty, as well as a powerful means for transferring this belief of certainty to others. A consequence to using this method, however, was the loss of the dialogical approach found in Plato's Socratic dialogues. In that approach, one learned, through the dialectical practice of the weighing of probabilities, a use of reason that was more interactive and oral and, therefore, much more ambiguous, contingent, and uncertain. The ambiguity, contingency, and uncertainty found in dialogical reasoning were characteristics that the Puritans sought to extinguish due, in part, to their anxiety ridden psychological makeup, which was tied to the Calvinist theological system of the elect (Emerson, 1977; Ong, 1958).

Ong (1958) suggested that such mapping presentations made sense to the Puritan congregation, for through the standardization brought on by printing, more and more diagrammatic systems of knowledge became available, literally changing the way individuals thought during the 1500s (Eisenstein, 1993; Ong, 1958). When the minister or schoolmaster handed out a Ramist map for the congregation or classroom to use as a means to follow along with his sermon or lecture, understanding what was spoken no longer developed dialogically between minister and congregation or teacher and student. Instead, mapped knowledge was to be "looked" at and followed along with silently and individually as the clergy or teacher instructed the congregation or classroom.

The Puritans' Ramist shift, away from understanding through dialogue to understanding by means of prescribed, charted-out systems of spiritual teachings or classroom disciplines, became part of the macrocosm of institutions—from family to church to higher learning and even to business dealings (Morgan, 1988; Ong, 1971). In fact, institutional consistency and interdependence was part of the larger process of moving the individual Puritan from one symbolic moment to the next, each step structuring the worldview by instructing (always in Ramist didactic form) the individual. For the colonial Puritans, schools were not the sole proprietor of education.

Each of the Puritan institutions had its educational function. The family provided the first bit of mechanics, specifically the vernacular language, priming the child to learn Latin, the formal language of schooling and the learned (Eisenstein, 1993; Kaufmann, 1999). But by no means were New England Puritans of one mind on this matter. Puritans perceived a child as one created in sin, with a tendency to be sinful and to feed off primitive impulses.

A parent who did not begin to disseminate the most basic principles of a Calvinist existence, in which evil must be identified and eradicated not only within one's soul but within all institutions as well, made it difficult for the schoolmaster and preacher later on. By the time the child reached 6 or 7 years of age, it was time for school:

Nothing, then, was more natural than the Puritan argument that young sons [we are dealing with a highly patriarchal culture, which continues in schooling to this day] armed with incipient literacy and elementary grasp of the basic notions of godly Protestantism, should be sent to the local school. It was but another step along the road to godliness. (Morgan, 1988, p. 171)

The schoolmaster was the linchpin between the household and the pulpit, each one serving a didactic function of guiding the Puritan individual through each institutional existence so that the nation as a whole could continue its sacred/secular journey toward building a New Jerusalem (Kaufmann, 1999; Morgan, 1988). Morgan (1988) wrote that the Ramist method enabled each institutional "teacher" to break down knowledge into its simplest parts and transmit it, especially to the young adolescent entering Harvard:

> Given the intellectual achievement of most grammar school students, it would seem reasonable to conclude that Ramism at this level was intended to provide a proper outlook concerning the value of empirical knowledge for those who were soon to enter apprenticeships, easier comprehension of basic logic and rhetoric for the few who would continue to the university, and greater access to comprehension of the Scriptures for all who sought salvation. (p. 86)

In the more traditional educational halls of Harvard, Ramism was the skeletal frame for the educational system called *technologia,* which was intended to reach not only the clergy but also the lay student, who made up about 50% of the student population. Ramism fit easily within the framework of the notion of *technologia,* for the assumption was that teaching and learning were "technical" acts of transmission and application of formalized method. The Puritans took the Greek notion of *techne,* meaning skill or art—as in the skill one achieved over time in making shoes or pottery—and added logia to it, thereby producing the study of a skill or art. For the Puritans, such training was to result in *eupraxia,* the art of right living, which for the Puritans meant the integration and balance of human reason and spiritual faith transmitted to all through the Ramist curriculum maps and method (Scott, 2000).

   In a connection to Ramism and the usefulness of this method as a kind of compendium or encyclopedic approach to ordering and transmitting knowledge, as represented at Harvard by Alsted's *Enyclopedia,* the Puritan circle of integrated knowledge was also referred to as "encyclopedia." Puritan theologian William Ames, who wrote *Technometria,* another one of the main texts at Harvard and Yale during the 18th century, defined *technologia* as the

> precognition of all the arts which adequately circumscribes the boundaries and ends of all the arts and of every art. . . . The comprehension of all those arts by which things emanate from the Es Primum [First Being] and return again to him is called Encyclopedia, whose first link of the circular chain is logic and the last theology. (quoted in Scott, 2000, p. 3)

Scott argued that the Puritans did not think encyclopedias a reference but a circle of knowledge in which one not only mastered scholarship in an academic discipline but also integrated that knowledge with one's activity in life. The Ramus method of ordering and transmitting knowledge was appropriated by those writing many of the textbooks used at Harvard, not only those including the already mentioned texts of Alsted and Ames, but alsoJon Comenius's *Physicae ad Lumen Divinum Reformatae* synopsis and Richardson's *Logicians Schoolmaster.*

During the 18th century, the old scholastic trivium and quadrivium from which these texts emerged eventually gave way to new subjects of study, including history, modern languages and literature, mathematics and experimental science, and finally the social sciences. However, such a shift toward the so-called "new learning" did not change the practices through which these subjects were ordered and transmitted.

And, as Puritanism dispersed into denominationalism, meaning the fragmentation of one Protestant theology into a variety of subtly different ones, each forming its own group consciousness but each adhering to certain generalized Protestant beliefs, the notion of education shifted. A balance between reason and inner piety was lost, especially by the mid-to-late 19th century, when a national consciousness was believed to have been defined by a nascent group interested in reforming the social landscape in its own image, a Puritan impulse (Mead, 1977).

However, for the urban Protestant middle class, which lived mostly in large Midwest and Northeastern cities and had a direct lineage to old Puritan families, education was expanded to encompass all Americans. As such, the Ramus construct of pedagogy and curriculum, based on a "plain speaking" explanation, became even more pervasive. This privileging of reason as framed within a Ramean context, now incorporated with a social scientific and technical construct, was embedded within the general educational discourse when schools were instituted on a mass scale. Education was still the way to salvation, was still the means of preserving the errand impulse and the American identity. But for the urban Protestant middle class, this translated into social salvation and the imposition of a morality as defined by leaders of their group, who were now participating more and more in the nontheological discourses gaining popularity at the time.

Due to a generalized pantheism (Dawson, 1984) in which America was still perceived as a Christian nation with a cultural mission, the urban Anglo-Protestant middle class now expressed the errand in ways that concentrated on methods of control, via reason, more so than personal salvation. However, the Puritan cultural trajectory and rhetorical methods of bringing the individual into the institutional remained embedded within the American consciousness and system.

4

Inheriting the Errand: Hopes and Fears of the Anglo-Protestant Middle Class

> Thus our large cities are a kind of biological furnace, which in the end consumes the lives supplied to it, in order to obtain the product in trade, science, and art. —*Henry Ling Taylor (1892, p. 45)*

FOR THE symbolic narrative of the errand into the wilderness to sustain solidarity and power over the imagination of mainstream America, a periodic recovery and renewal must take place. Such an event occurs when the errand is perceived to have diverged from its original trajectory by a loss of commonly held understandings of the content and purpose of the American identity.

The sudden uncertainty of identity and purpose is usually coupled with external tensions, such as the immigration of "alien" cultures that intensify the sense of doubt. In response to these tears in the fabric of America's grand mission, the linguistic terrain must convert the symbolism into a gesture that evokes the visceral passions and moral willingness to submit to the metanarrative. If the ritual of renewal fails to deliver a reinvigorated symbolic narrative that captures the moral sensibilities of mainstream America, the symbols and hence the sense of American historical and transcendent purpose would tremble, then transform the identity of the country into something very different.

Such a major re-presentation of the errand came to pass during the late 1800s and early 1900s. This was a time when urbanization, industrialization, and immigration culminated in great ambivalence due to a perceived fracture of moral certainty and national purpose, instigating a moral reform movement based on a belief in providential design. The errand impulse was appropriated and acted on by the emerging American Anglo-Protestant, urban, middle class, specifically those involved in the professions. This nascent collection of urbanites redefined American identity in language that suited their own desires and concepts of American destiny (Bercovitch, 1993; Dawson, 1984). They perceived themselves as the heart, soul, and intellect of America, a condition that carried with it a sense of possession and right to reform, reinvent, and remember national identity and morality. Because the errand narrative was symbolic and hence flexible, the emerging urban corpus slipped easily into constructing the world in terms of a moral crisis that only it could resolve. The symbolic identity could change in specific content and language, such as shifting from employing errand terminology to articulate America's destiny to using the modern terms Manifest Destiny and Progress as the driving force in the spread across the continent. However, the drama of the ritual and renewal narrative persisted.

As the fledgling group of capitalist-minded urbanites faced the entrance of a new century and a change in material conditions, specifically in the institutions of family, church, and school, they responded as the Puritan habit of thought had trained them—reconcile or erase all of the uncertainty and anxiety inherent in society. Each institution was supposedly still responsible for moving the individual into adult institutional life, but because of changes in the social conditions of family and church, one institution began to take on a greater and greater role in this process. This process was constructed around creating a different kind of visible saint and American identity, that of the "moral," sober, hard worker whose purpose was to serve the economy, which in turn would make America the kind of world power the colonial Puritans could only imagine in their jeremiads and scholarly productions. The institution of schooling became the means to create this individual by emphasizing basic moral inculcation and knowledge transmission—operations that could be measured and controlled through the technocratic discourse schools now valued over the more indirect literal/figural Puritan narrative. An effect was that education became narrowed and restricted to the space and function of public schools (Bullough, 1974).

Control as method (Doll, 1998), important to the colonial Puritans as one part of the overall educational purpose, became *the* means to reproduce middle-class culture. An effect was that the spiritually trans-formative aspect of education privileged by the colonial Puritans was excised and placed solely within the institutions of family or church. However, this happened just at the moment when the institutions of family and church were undergoing massive transformations and were less capable of handling this task, which served to increase the impor-tance of school as moral inculcator and the site in which uncertainty could be measured and controlled. Just as with their colonial predeces-sors, the Anglo-Protestant middle class believed that as the world was a chaotic place, it was their mission to give it order. For both the colonial Puritans and their cultural heirs, the Anglo-Protestant, Northeastern, urban middle class, the metaphorical and literal place of the city was perceived as both opportunity and potential destroyer of the great errand.

AN AMBIVALENT URBAN MIDDLE CLASS

Members of the Protestant, urban middle class shared a sense that the cities, mostly in the Northeast, were material manifestations of the symbolic "city upon the hill." Cities were theirs to build and protect. Although this urban middle class was not much more than a loose aggregate, its participants were becoming intently aware of a profes-sional connectedness from which emerged a unique identity and within which was harbored shared social impulses:

> Covering too wide a range to form a tightly knit group, it divided into two broad categories. One included those with strong professional aspirations in such fields as medicine, law, economics, administration, social work, and architecture. The second comprised specialists in business, in labor, and in agriculture awakening both to their distinctiveness and to their ties with similar people in the same occupation.
>
> In fact, consciousness of unique skills and functions, an awareness that came to mold much of their lives, characterized all members of the class. They demonstrated it by a proud identification as lawyers and teachers, by a determination to improve the contents of medicine or the proce-dures of a particular business, bound by an eagerness to join others like themselves in a craft union, professional organization, trade organiza-tions, or agricultural cooperative. (Wiebe, 1967, p. 112)

However, at the end of the 19th century, a pervading sense of social disruption and transformation provided plenty of moral dilemmas for a Protestant middle-class mind to mull over. More often than not, a response to these ruminations was ambivalence, a persistent state of simultaneous hope and despair.

Signs of hope and opportunity were everywhere. Cities were becoming the sites of social influence and industrial and economic growth, which was perceived as part of the natural process of progress, and there was a sense by the Anglo-Protestant, urban, middle class that they had inherited the errand and were to preserve and broaden America's role as world redeemer. As a sense of being best suited to steer America into the future began to increase in intensity, the old colonial Puritan moral vigor for reform took hold:

> Finally the ability to see how their talents meshed with others in a national scheme encouraged them to look outward confidently instead of furtively. As much as any other trait, an earnest desire to remake the world upon their private models testified to the deep satisfaction accompanying this revolution in identity. (Wiebe, 1967, p. 113)

In effect, the errand into the wilderness was transformed into Manifest Destiny and the mission of Progress:

> Insofar as the kingdom was conceived in social terms the faith in its coming was transformed into a belief in progress. The judgment was really past. It had occurred in a democratic revolution. The life now lived in the land of promise was regarded as the promised life and no greater bliss seemed possible for men than was afforded by the extension of American institutions to all the world. . . . The self-congratulatory tone appeared even in the youthful Bushnell, who took it for "granted that complete Protestantism is pure Christianity," while Protestantism in its complete form is congregationalism and congregationalism is the author of republicanism. "We are the depositories of that light," he cried, "which is to illuminate the world." (Niebuhr, 1966, p. 245)

To insure that such moral conditions would continue to prevail, the Protestant urban middle class set out to remake the city by compelling others to follow an old Puritan maxim, "doing right in a world that does wrong" (Morgan, 1944). To do right meant to impose a will and a form on the world, to find its rightful order ("form controls matter"). The operative word in the phrase for the middle class became control—of themselves and of others (Blumin, 1991; Tyack & Hansot, 1982).

The assumption was that if their will, their sense of morality, could be imposed, then variables that emerge from historical transformations and from individuals proceeding through moral questioning could be contained. In other words, their morality could be institutionalized. And as the etymology of "institution" suggests, this is a two-way cut. To institute is to set up, to establish, to put into place. But to institute also is to confine (i.e., to institutionalize a mental patient), which I extend to confining the common faith, that of the errand impulse and symbol and the notion of a national identity, to an institution intent on mass control, such as schooling (a meaning that gained credence in the early 1900s). Those living in the burgeoning cities in the Northeast did not view what they were doing in such terms. They, for the most part, willed themselves to see the grandeur of the new "city upon a hill."

In 1894, King Gillette, inventor and promoter of the famous Gillette razor, wrote *The Human Drift*. In this book he celebrated this move to institutionalize the middle-class moral narrative and framework, which spoke not necessarily of a city upon a hill but of a Utopia instead. For Gillette, a Utopian society corresponded to the urban, middle-class sense of looking into the crystal ball of America's future and seeing its own reflection.

Through the application of the language and methods of science, a discourse gaining more and more credence among the general population, America would again throw light upon the world:

> There are clouds upon the horizon of thought, and the very air we breathe is pregnant with life that foretells the birth of a wonderful change. Darkness will cover the whole dome that encircles the earth, the storm will break, and from the travail of nature reason will have its birth and assume its sway o'er the minds of men. (Gillette, 1894, title page)

For many urban, middle-class Protestants, Gillette represented all the positive moral attributes the merger of Christianity and capitalism could produce: efficiency, hard work, soberness, business competition skills, individualistic economic motives that result in the betterment of society, a sense of secular endeavors being driven by divine providence and, above all, self-control.

However, equally intense pitfalls and anxieties sat at the other end of the spectrum and counterbalanced much of the optimism: fears of material loss due to a boom and bust economy that gripped America throughout the latter 19th century; fears that somehow the cultural identity of America, as becoming defined by the urban, Protestant middle class, would be forsaken and forgotten if the massive flow of immigrants with unfamiliar cultural habits and expressions were not socialized into the ways of its errand; fears that the "traditional" family no longer existed because of industrialization, with an effect of a generalized push to locate another institution to incorporate the duties previously held by the family (specifically the father); fear of the growing conflict between labor and employers, each claiming the mantle of true American righteousness; fears that the morphology of cultural existence was shifting faster than the urban middle-class Protestants could control and direct, a job they deemed their responsibility. Such shifts produced anxiety, a state of being that indicated a need for clarification and alleviation.

A litany of "ations,"—immigration, urbanization, industrialization —were the new wildernesses encroaching on the growing cities. In that steady Puritan logic, the content (matter) of the wilderness had two simultaneous possibilities: something evil and savage in need of taming and controlling, and/or something good and hopeful, a place through which progress (the secular word for God's plan, or sometimes even God Himself) could sustain itself. For example, in 1892, Henry Ling Taylor, a medical authority, surveyed the city and decided that its unrural-like ways of life perpetuated sinful temptations for adults and youths alike. In an urban jeremiad, written in a discourse in which the interest in technology and natural science was becoming evident (e.g., the city as biological furnace), Taylor (1892) wrote that a loss of moral compass in such a chaotic site as the city certainly leads to failing physical and mental health:

> Conspicuous factors in modern life are the extreme specialization of pursuits and occupations, tending to narrow and restrict experience, and the herding together of dense masses of population in large cities, toward which the more venturesome and ambitious individuals tend to gravitate, and where large opportunities are provided, only at the cost of more strenuous competitions, and in many respects less favorable hygienic conditions.
>
> Success is paid for, both directly and remotely, in pounds of flesh. (p. 44)

Alarm over city dwelling and its sinful temptations that could seduce an otherwise good Protestant middle-class individual presented a rough moral terrain to navigate. Such complex internal issues then functioned to divert attention away from this difficulty to other content more easily situated, imposed on, and contained—immigrants.

IMMIGRANTS AND THE URBAN PROTESTANT MIDDLE-CLASS RESPONSE

Immigrants provided the middle class with clearly identifiable categories from which to differentiate it and define its own errand morality. This new wave of immigrants embodied all the characteristics that would come to constitute immorality. Also, they had no rank, no claims to an American legacy. In swift fashion, the new immigrants fell with the province of the Puritan/urban, middle-class Protestant impulse to reform.

The welcoming arms of the Statue of Liberty, that symbol of America as the world's asylum, exacted a price on those accepting her embrace: Leave your cultural baggage on the ship. The extent of the payment is evident in the meanings of the word asylum: "1. An inviolable place of refuge and protection. . . . Sanctuary. . . . 4: An institution for the relief or care of the destitute or afflicted and especially the *insane*" (*Webster's New College Dictionary,* 1995, p. 55, emphasis mine).

Cotton Mather first introduced the notion of America as an asylum in his 1689 book, *Work Upon the Ark.* Mather celebrated "New England as a sanctuary and ship of state which enjoyed special protection and offered asylum to refugees" (Blanke, 1983, p. 221).

> For the Puritans, especially near the end of the Colonial Period, the rhetoric of asylum became very popular . . . because it combined the religious concern of the Puritans with the political concern of all British Americans. It allowed them to be sympathetic with persecuted Protestants everywhere and with revolutionaries. By offering their land as an asylum, they could advance their mission without getting into trouble with powerful nations abroad. (Blanke, 1983, p. 221)

However, when these images sank into the imaginations of those not of the same cultural stock, mostly non-Protestant southern Europeans who in the late 1800s sought to escape hunger, joblessness, and hope-lessness in their own countries, the urban Protestant middle-class American response could be called schizophrenic. Like a pendulum, it swung back and forth from displaying open arms to xenophobic cries for legislation to stanch the flow of immigration. The pristine errand of transforming the wilderness into a sanctuary might prosper with the addition of more bodies, but it also might collapse from an invasion of those perceived as the European afflicted and insane (to incorporate the double meaning of asylum). These immigrants were different from the first wave of immigrants that came over in the 19th century.

Higham (1984) compared the American urban scene to a Tower of Babel:

> Whereas the First Immigration had been entirely white and predominantly English speaking, the Second brought a Babel of tongues and an array of complexions ranging from the blond Scandinavian through the swarthy south Italian to the West Indian Negro. And whereas the First Immigration had been very largely Protestant, the second was heavily Catholic from the outset; and by the end of the century it was increasingly Jewish and Eastern Orthodox. (p. 21)

Such pronounced differences provided the urban Protestant middle class with striking phenomena on which to focus its moral anxiety. Many immigrant groups who could not or who refused to immediately assimilate fueled urgent moral concerns. The urban middle class fully expected all immigrants to assimilate over time, by force if necessary. This faith (or willfulness) not only issued forth from the Puritan ideals of morality and virtue as applicable to all mankind, but also from the general acceptance of the Enlightenment rationale of plural groups coming to believe and operate from universal ideals necessary to propagate a free republic. This is not to separate out the Puritans from the Enlightenment, for many Puritan intellectuals were involved in finding rational methods by which to best live one's life. A difference is that colonial Puritans applied Enlightenment thought, for the most part, to the individual search rather than to a search to determine the morality for all.

Urban cultural leaders worried that immigrant numbers would expand to the point of overwhelming the urban middle class and could wrestle away control of America's destiny away just as the middle class was getting comfortable in its social position. New York City presents a striking, though extreme, example of this:

In 1890 four out of five New Yorkers were foreign-born, a higher propor-
tion than any other city in the world. New York had twice as many Irish as
Dublin, as many Germans as Hamburg, and half as many Italians as
Naples. (Tindall, 1988, p. 824)

Higham (1984) described the effect of this on middle-class Protestant
Americans:

> The mounting sense of danger—even dispossession—among millions
> of native-born white Protestants . . . is not hard to understand. A people
> whose roots were in the towns and farms of the early republic saw great
> cities coming more and more under the control of strangers whose
> speech and values were not their own. A people who unconsciously iden-
> tified Protestantism with Americanism saw Catholic voters and urban
> bosses gaining control of the industrialized states. . . . In reaction, the
> older Americans mounted a cultural counter-offensive through the pro-
> hibition movement, immigration restriction, and a sharpened racism.
> (p. 48)

For many, the solution to the immigrant "dilemma" was to fall into
an implicit emphasis on the latter meaning of the word asylum. Immigrants could continue to enter American ports, but they would have to
submit their children to a new identity through the imposition of a prescribed morality provided by the institution of public schools. In fact,
national educational leaders in the late 1800s, such as William Torrey
Harris, Charles Eliot, and Nicholas Murray Butler, each drew a direct
correlation, through the use of social scientific surveys, between the lack
of schooling and crime. This appealed greatly to the anxious urban middle class that still wanted to believe in "equal opportunity for each man;
a test of individual merit; wealth as a reward for virtue; credit for hard
work, frugality, and dedication; a premium upon efficiency; a government that minded its own business; a belief in society's progressive
improvement" (Wiebe, 1967, p. 136).

But these traditions appeared to be mocked by the actions of certain wealthy individuals—men who claimed to live according to these
moral principles even as, to many of the urban middle class, they trans-
gressed such national community boundaries (Dawson, 1984). Despite
the Puritan moral maxim of a man's material gain as a sign of God's
grace, most Protestant middle-class Americans could no longer blindly
accept one man deserving such abundance. Wiebe (1967) summed up

the Protestant middle-class sentiment: "No just God had given Rocke-feller his money, whatever the man said" (p. 134). However, vexations for the urban middle-class's moral indignation arose from an ironic reality: No one could actually prove the very wealthy did not possess what the middle class considered appropriate moral values. The courts inter-preted the acts of aggrandizement by the letter of the law, which upheld their wealth. And because the urban middle class had invested much moral capital into the very legal system that was supposed to preserve the moral structure of the community, its hands were tied.

Although this tension has never abated (it remains today), it did com-pel an intensive exploration of how such now questionable excesses of the very discourses embraced by most Protestants could be contained. In fact, the desire to "contain" and "direct" provides a clue to what aspect of the colonial Puritan symbolic heritage emerged as the guiding mode of moral thought during the late 1800s and early 1900s—the old Puri-tan (as derived from the Reformation) maxim of control. In other words, a moral adult was one who practiced behavioral control, of him-self or herself and of others when placed in a position of authority. Con-trol had different effects, as well as demands, that depended not only on one's cultural legacy but one's gender. For schools to be successful in imposing moral forms, the "natural" male and female tendencies had to be revealed and explicated. In the late 1800s, it was accepted that God had given each sex certain biological differences that affected their be-havior. How society would decide to employ those differences to benefit the cultural mission of America, and the ways in which each individual would come to accept the role that best suited his or her "natural" attrib-utes, became the function of schools.

The errand was inextricably bound to moral behavior of each indi-vidual. What was and was not moral behavior depended on one's gen-der. Each gender, it was believed, possessed different biological impulses that dictated the need for different methods and forms of control.

CONTROL AND PROTESTANT
GENDER ROLES

Rotundo (1987) identified three basic masculine models given currency in the American Protestant discourse: Masculine Achiever, Christian Gentleman, and Masculine Primitive. Rotundo wrote that the Masculine Achiever was naturally active and dynamic. "As one lawyer put it: 'Man is made for action and the bustling scenes of moving life, and not the poetry or romance of existence.' Activity—strong, aggressive action —formed an important part of the ideal of the Masculine Achiever" (p. 36).

The idea of the Masculine Achiever is threaded through the gender discourse of the late 1800s and early 1900s and is part of the network of notions, including the liberal capitalistic self-made man interested in material gain and self improvement; a state of *being* necessary for even greater material success and social prominence. The language of the Masculine Achiever conveyed a need, at least in public, for a reasoned approach in attaining his desires. One was not to allow certain possible emotional responses, such as compassion and mercy, to impede one's ultimate ends (Rotundo, 1987). Freedom was self-reliance, even a form of self-containment. In this ideal the ends justified the means, although the means did have certain parameters. Certain emotions were considered necessary to express whereas others needed dominating and burying.

Presented as an opposition to this was the Christian Gentleman, categorized as one interested in maintaining communal order against the "threat" of economic individualism run amuck (Rotundo, 1987). This ideal stressed love, kindness, and compassion. However, before turning to such external attributes, a man must first conquer his inner desires. He must achieve complete control over his body and faculties: "By calling for such total self-control, the ideal of the Christian Gentleman demanded a conquest of the inner environment" (Rotundo, 1987, p. 40). Although the Protestant urban middle class gradually delineated these categories to establish desirable moral attributes, and in the process developed two opposing roles, such constructions inevitably returned to the same moral point inherited from Puritan thought—the impulse of self-control. Nature had to be conquered.

Even the Masculine Achiever, driven by the inward desire for external material and social gain (part of the natural animality of man as understood by the social Darwinistic discourse of the era [Hofstadter, 1959]), had to subjugate himself to a structure of reasoned control. On the same continuum, the Christian Gentleman had to conquer his inward state of depravity before entering into worldly matters. Although one could argue that the Masculine Achiever employed reason to justify inner gratification and the Christian Gentleman wanted to conquer inner gratification for a greater purpose, both worked from the theory of the need to control certain naturalized forces perceived as wicked if allowed to emerge unfettered.

In other words, as with most constructed oppositions, one does not exist without the other and as such is inextricably linked to the other in ways that make it impossible to separate. Despite efforts to separate the ideals in neat and clean ways by imposing categories and privileging one value over another, when applied to concrete circumstances, these categories collapsed into the common denominator of control.

However, there was another competing ideal that contradicted the others: Masculine Primitive. The Masculine Primitive reveled in his body and his aggressiveness. Anger became a possible response where before it was thoroughly disdained and feared. Self-control was ideal for most situations, but anger, wild fury, and passion became perceived as natural inclinations of the male. Such bodily outbursts were necessary at times, according to this discourse, which complemented the "findings" of those perpetuating social Darwinism as scientific and applicable to all living beings. This discourse also gave credence to the cultural assumption that man was basically depraved and occupied with a violent nature. Around this ideal emerged sporting ways that celebrated such violent possibilities. In fact, collegiate sports grew out of this discourse during the 1850s (Rotundo, 1987; Stearns, 1987).

Again, to try and reconcile the seeming disparity in the ideals, the notion of channeling emotions toward preferred goals was privileged. In other words, self-discipline was ideal, but because anger had become viewed as a legitimate, naturalized male way, it had to be routed in an appropriate manner. Stearns (1987) wrote that in the late 19th century, anger was not necessarily bad as long as it was sublimated in terms of sporting, academic, or economic competition:

> For, in men, anger could now be good as well as bad. Not in raw form, no one pulled back from disapproval of literal displays of personal temper. But, properly channeled, anger was a useful spur. Indeed, its absence was to be lamented. (Stearns, p. 81)

Emotion, presented in certain ways, provided the impetus for higher goals.

The tension between the different ideals of male morality could not be resolved. The ideals did, however, lend an available context by which to cope and to continue to try and clarify moral matters. In other words, each ideal had its function for the American Protestant as each was accepted as a natural impulse. Despite tensions between each ideal, as long as certain moral imperatives of self-control guided an individual, complemented by the accepted notion of Progress (from which social salvation emerges), and did not threaten the existing social system, most criticisms failed to penetrate the cultural armor.

In what now appears as tortured logic, males could not be trusted to preserve the highest moral ideals—the cultural vision of the errand and the Protestant middle-class identity as the American identity—because of their nature. Self-control could only contain the beast, not kill it. As such, the beast proved to be a constant threat to the higher moral goals spelled out by the current social milieu. In what appears as another contradiction, the "natural" forces that men supposedly harbored within their very souls, the violent forces that endangered the moral errand, were the very ones that cultural leaders prescribed as necessary for the formation and the continued progress of the errand. God ordained that the Puritans inscribe the wilderness, to take it for their own (conquer) and transform it (a very aggressive, supposedly male action and process).

For the 19th-century middle-class Protestant, the divine order was not only to spread out across the West but also to move into the city and impose his or her reflection on it. This wander–conquer lust, if you will, so dominated the notions of what constituted male inclinations that many realized the danger in males losing their self-control and grip on higher reasoning. "Man" needed tempering beyond self-control. He needed an example by which to live. He also had to have a place in which those inclinations could not dominate, where the so-called higher moral inclinations could be given space to grow.

In a remarkable advertisement for the logic of polar oppositions, if men are by nature aggressive, then women are not. If work is where competition and aggression bubble up, even though controlled, then home is a haven away from such pressures. And if home is such a place, then the home is best suited for the woman, or, more specifically, the mother. Woman as mother became the keeper of the hearth, the guardian of all that was not the depraved state of man, which threatened the Protestant existence with its destructive sensibility (even though such a state was necessary to sustain God's plan for America). Woman represented the nurturer, the purifier, and all ideals embedded in that category. From the home was to emerge the child who grows into adult-hood and who, according to the symbolism of the errand, must embody the identity of America before completing the maturation process. The mother had to control the moral forms of the home, and later, the schools. It is noteworthy that the social-scientific discourse, despite its claim to moral neutrality, had the effect of giving credence to the desig-nation of woman as more moral, more pure, more good than man and, therefore, placed woman in the position to assume the roles in society that would protect these very assumptions (Conway, 1971).

By the late 1800s, the obligation of salvation fell heavily on the mother as the father spent more and more time outside the home labor-ing in factories or working as a professional. The home in the early Puri-tan era was a place where both mother, father, daughter, and son often worked side by side, thus maintaining, for good or bad, a family's sense of work as a form of piety, an extension of the worship that occurred in the same home. However, with the advent of industrialization, this con-nectedness altered. The home became the domain of the mother, not in the sense of the mother having full authority over the household, but in the sense that the home became a burden of the mother to maintain and to nurture:

> As men and women drifted father apart in the workplace, the social roles of the sexes became more distinct. The "cult of true womanhood," based on the Victorian understanding of woman as the model of purity, piety, and domesticity, separated women from men and their world. Women who hoped to accomplish "masculine" goals such as education or a career were limited by social expectations of their feminine nature; and men were separated from domestic activities because of their different "char-acter." Although men might continue to consider themselves patriarchs of the home, they seemed unable to exercise that authority. Now the mother, according to cultural norms, was expected to nurture the family. (McDannell, 1986, pp. 7–8)

Although such expectations bothered those who recognized the lim-iting prospect of this gender role, many women found themselves un-willing to resist because of certain "material" improvements in their lives: "The cost of middle class domesticity had been a high one, but few Americans, even those most at the mercy of nineteenth-century capitalism, would be willing to turn away from the dream of a 'proper home' and family" (McDannell, 1986, p. 10).

However, just as women became the guardians and moral leaders of the family, the family found itself in a precarious position. Its traditional cultural role weakened. In fact, national educational leaders provided compelling arguments for an expanded role of public schools due, in part, to the dramatic changes in the family structure during industrialization. These national figures, such as Nicholas Murray Butler, Charles Eliot, and William Torrey Harris, asserted that public schools could function as the institution most able to guide a child through the embodiment process. Schools could preserve the moral imperative. So just as women emerged as the guardians of the hearth, other discourses critiqued this domain as incapable of inculcating the child into earthly morality. In fact, the home and family were believed prone to spoil the child in light of the mother's more dominant role there. In effect, the logic put forth was that women were basically weak and could not control the child without the help of male experts providing strict methods of child rearing (White, 1969). Once women moved in the direction of the "teaching" field, professional males quickly created programs to prepare these women to teach as directed, another example of the patriarchal social constructions of the colonial Puritans persevering even as the language of social science was employed rather than the earlier privileged metaphorical language.

CHURCH AND FAMILY FRAGMENTATION

By the late 1800s and early 1900s, America had transformed into a pan-sectarian nation with a broad-based Protestantism to which one specific theology could no longer provide simple answers or arbitrate conflicts. Protestantism was now so expansive that it functioned more as a set of cultural assumptions than as anything so specific as a theology—assumptions that defined the urban middle-class sense of national identity and its corresponding social order. As Mead (1977) wrote:

> [D]uring the course of the nineteenth century the denominations ... easily came to sanctify the ideals and spirit of the rising industrial, acquisitive bourgeois society until by the end of the century there was almost complete identification of Christianity with the "American way of life" until, as Henry May put it, "In 1876 Protestantism presented a massive, almost unbroken front in its defense of the social status quo." (p. 98)

This is not to say that Americans did not take their religion seriously. One's cultural community, even in the city, still gave the church central importance. However, a problem for the American urban middle-class Protestants at this time was the internal competition among theologies that emerged during the Reformation (Mead, 1977). American Protestant theologies ranged from extreme Calvinism, a direct legacy of the Puritans, to the increasingly popular Methodism (a much milder Protestant form). In the public realm of social reform, it became obvious that no one church or theology, at this period in American history, was suited to supply a morality in any formalized manner to either newly arrived immigrant children or a generation of Anglo-Protestant children (Kaestle, 1984). As discussed in earlier chapters, no one theology could ever assume such a role, for the very nature of Protestantism, as it developed in America, was the possibility of local autonomy and personal interpretation, although each was linked to the unifying symbolic structure of the errand into the wilderness.

No longer did families center their lives around, or within, for that matter, the church to the extent that they did before. Church was becoming a place to go on Sundays, with only its rhetorical residue sticking to the urban crowd walking to a new haven that even the church found difficult to control—the home (Cross, 1975). America could not locate the day-to-day functions of preserving the present, as the place and time that history had naturally progressed to, in the hands of an institution that had such limited access to the child (Cross, 1975).

The belief that the amount of access to a child correlates to the worth of an institution as a moral inculcator reveals urban Protestant middle-class Americans' general sense of morality as a matter of control. The more time adults spend with children, the more children could be exposed to culturally accepted adult ways of interacting. Hence, a desired effect was that children would less likely develop their own ethical mechanisms of interacting with peers. Children were to be prepared to live as adults and not to work through the particulars of confronting the so-called moral dilemmas that would develop in their own unique age group. The moral problems of the adult world were considered universal and, therefore, applied to the child's world as well.

Such assumptions about the nature of children, about the anxiety of wanting to sustain a present vision of a desired future by placing the burden on the shoulders of the next generation, reveal how another American institution in transition caught the attention of many post-

Civil War thinkers—the family. However, the conventional notion of what constituted a family was in decline. The family, as it was beginning to exist, was in no position to offer any formalized way of preserving the future as reenvisioned by the nascent urban middle class. Economic realities that emerged out of industrialization, bolstered by American Protestant religious support of the institutions that came to be during this historical transformation, tended to fragment the "traditional" family. Even though social rhetoric constituted by the symbolic framework of America attached seminal importance to the institution of the family, it was evident to many that to hand over so much cultural power to a domain no longer unified and almost wholly associated with what was defined as feminine was not practical. In effect, to many there was a fear that the child, under the hands of women for most of the day, would be spoiled and would lose his "natural" male tendencies; that the boy would become weak.

The family shifted from a community-based extended family in which kinfolk and neighbors participated in the raising of the children in preparation for rural life, to one of urban disorientation and division of labor. The father left home for long periods of time to work at an office or factory. The mother assumed a multitude of roles that had the effect of actually diverting her away from the act of nurturing, despite the greater emphasis placed on the female as a natural nurturer, a tension that has still not subsided (McDannell, 1986; Wiebe, 1967). Few extended family members could step in to preserve the prior methods of child rearing because in the city, rarely could such a communal network develop (Bullough, 1974; McDannell, 1986). The Protestant urban middle class was caught in a dangerous state of constant transition, opposite to how rural life was perceived. Rural life was stable and certain. Whether such statements actually corresponded with any kind of statistical reality did not matter. People felt changes in their lives.

From this impulse to control and formulate what would happen in the future by finding and developing ways that more "accurately" expressed what the new urban Protestant middle class was experiencing, cultural leaders realized the difficulty, if not the impossibility, of locating the moral burden of America's future in such a transitional and fragmented institution as the family.

What occurred concerning the family was two-fold. The significance of the family as the beginning point of education remained. However, the expectations of the family to fully educate the child were erased.

Many feared that to hand over all rhetoric and cultural educating power to women would actually stifle certain natural attributes of men— competition, aggressiveness, rage—that in the correct quantities were necessary for the progress of the American identity, or better, actually gave the American identity its distinctiveness and redemptive power (Rotundo, 1987). In fact, a preponderance of child-rearing magazines and journals began to appear, supplying step-by-step processes developed by experts for parents to use to elevate the child born in the state of nature (meaning animality) into an enlightened state (McDannell, 1986; White, 1969). But some interpreted this as an effort to remove from the mother power over the children by prescribing ahead of time what she could or should do in terms of raising her children. In one way, the methods appeared to substitute for an absent father.

No longer were parents expected by cultural leaders to employ their own methods and particularized understandings of their children. Parental responsibility was now restricted to imposing a set of moral maxims on the child. However, even this role was beginning to be absorbed by schools. During this time, due to compulsory attendance laws (Bullough, 1974) and the growth of kindergartens, schools gained more and more access to a child for longer periods of time (White, 1969). Kindergartens gained popularity due to the labors of Susan Blow and her colleague William Torrey Harris in the late 19th century, both of whom believed the child, the parents, the community, and the nation would be better served if schools were given the authority to direct the moral development of all American children.

More and more, educators celebrated, through local politics as well as through national academic journals, the possibility of public schools appropriating a broader cultural role (Troen, 1975). Public schools would preserve the moral imperative, an imperative translated as the control of and transmission to the child of cultural knowledge and not the transformation of the child. This coalesced around a burgeoning confidence in the belief that America had in some sense drawn more closely to the realization of its cultural mission. The "end" of history was near. Schools now had only to transmit the correct values. By embodying those values, a child would mature into a moral adult who would behave in an acceptable social manner. To function as a "normal" social being now translated as a state of being defined by the moral predisposition's of the urban, Anglo-Protestant middle class. The errand for the urban middle class was to create individuals willing to act in ways that would further guarantee a national identity as defined by this group.

The logic pursued placed the existing social system within the domain of God's intent and, as such, protected it from the vicissitudes of mankind's moral depravity. All that was left was to identify the morals that corresponded to the "needs" of the social system and transmit them as a form of knowledge. This discourse served those urban professionals responsible for regulating the quickly expanding public school systems across the nation, in that schools became a means of perpetuating middle-class habits and ways. This discourse based its effectiveness on the assumption that all humans were essentially the same in terms of behavior, which was perceived as the crux of morality. The moral expressions, as represented by the Protestant urban middle class, were to be imposed on all others. And beginning with this period in American history, if a behavior could be measured, then it could be easily categorized and valued and provided a method by which to achieve (Kliebard, 1992).

5

The New Discourses of Education: "Reason" to Preserve the Moral Imperative

One can safely assert that the teaching corps as a body, longs to be the means of turning the light into the souls of children so that no darkness shall thwart and hinder the upward climb.
—*Ella Flagg Young (1902, p. 41)*

WITH THE CLOSE of the Civil War, certain national issues had been decided and the nation looked toward the future with both hope and trepidation and an even greater sense of destiny. During this period, the inherited spiritualized impulses remained intact, although the language that conceptualized the desires of inscribing a moral identity on all shifted in emphasis from the internal to the external. Instead of each institution providing metaphorical narrative maps that acknowledged the uncertainty of individual existence and meaning, the Anglo-Protestant urban middle class fastened onto the claims of science and reason to wash away uncertainty. The belief was that the moral behaviors that constituted American middle-class identity could be empirically identified and transmitted in an instrumental and literal fashion.

Instead of creating individuals to reflect a national identity tied to God's providential design, fervent calls were heard demanding a national, more secular civil religion that would oversee the "business" of the nation (Bercovitch, 1975; Niebuhr, 1966), or what Tyack and Hansot (1982) called the "bureaucratization of redemption" (p. 32).

What also remained was the passionate psychological impulse to view education as the primary vehicle for preserving the new, yet still symbolic, narrative of national destiny. By the end of the 19th century, the self-chosen inheritors of the symbolic narrative decided that mass public schooling was a worthy institution in which to pour public funds. Not only was it believed that schools were the most adequate site to perpetuate, in children, this coalescing Northeastern, urban, Anglo-Protestant, middle-class identity, but schools also were considered vehicles by which to spread that moral sense of destiny to all those who followed different predispositions. It was certainly education for all, but an education that was quite calculated and narrow in scope. Although confident that the new American city was a near fulfillment of the symbolic narrative's representation of the "city upon a hill," the new middle class still fretted that all would be lost if the new wave of immigrants, who sounded and looked different, did not quickly embody their values. Just as Puritans utilized schooling as a means of instructing individuals in institutional ways, the same held true for the urban, Protestant middle class, although on a much larger scale.

Significant in this publicly funded effort to create mass public schooling was the continuation of the Ramist curricular methods of simplifying, ordering, and presenting the world through a "plain speaking" discourse. Ramism was well equipped for the needs of the emerging middle class, which wished to naturalize its explanation as to why America and all Americans should "look" and act like its members.

In effect, this "method," which for the colonial Puritans was a prominent though still ambiguous trajectory, became *the* discourse of instruction, a kind of "professionalization of knowledge" (Popkewitz, 1986, p. 7) employed by a growing number of professional, middle-class urbanites in the Northeast. The middle class could hide behind this discourse as it claimed neutrality and was located within the realm of the "expert" (Popkewitz, 1986). This discourse followed the rhetorical patterns set up by Ramus and suited the desire to separate the world into segments that could be easily measured, categorized, transmitted, and digested (Wiebe, 1967, 1969). It also matched the bureaucratic mentality of order and control that was determining how mass public schools would appear and operate during the late 19th and early 20th centuries (Callahan, 1962; Kaestle, 1984; White, 1969).

To forgo the balance between faith and reason struck by the colonial Puritans was to lose the more ambiguous elements of the symbolic narrative. The ambiguity had allowed the symbolic narrative to weather and adapt to social disruptions and changes in meaning. In other words, the discourse of school employed fewer humanistic metaphors and spiritual overtones in favor of a literal, technocratic language of objectivity and "reason," which was very much a part of colonial Puritan discourse, although tempered by a language of "faith." The Northeastern middle class collapsed "faith" into rationality and placed its "faith" in the analytic–technocratic rationale of efficiency and control (Callahan, 1962). The new mass public schools followed this path. As early as the late 19th century, Harvard president Charles Eliot called for an American curriculum to "champion the systematic development of reasoning power as the central function of the schools" (quoted in Kliebard, 1987, p. 11). He argued that reason provides a process of accurate observation, classification, and categorization, thereby directing the curriculum to instruct a student in the mental habit of expressing one's thoughts "clearly, concisely, and cogently." To do so was to believe that reason would reflect the natural world as it really was, which had an interesting effect on the more secular jeremiads beginning to pour out of the pens of the urban, middle-class professionals.

A social jeremiad no longer threatened God's wrath, but instead warned of a loss of power and standing in the material world. The power of persuasion remained, but the symbolic intent shifted drastically as the professional middle class believed that it had let go of the old, "silly" metaphors and beliefs and entered the new world of science and reason as the way for "form to control matter." The new professional middle class was confident that its position was the righteous core of American thought and possessed a morality that only needed transmitting, not interpreting. Moral questions, at the heart of the colonial Puritans religious impulse, no longer needed discussion. Adams (1918/1974) described this phenomenon, and the need to answer (and in the end the belief that all was answered) the moral questions once and for all:

> The religious instinct had vanished, and could not be revived. . . . That the most powerful emotion of man, next to the sexual, should disappear, might be a personal defect of his own; but that the most intelligent society, led by the most intelligent clergy, in the most moral conditions he ever knew, should have solved all the problems of the universe so thoroughly as to have quite ceased making itself anxious about the past or future, and should have persuaded itself that all the problems which had

convulsed human thought from earliest recorded time, were not worth
discussing, seemed to him the most curious social phenomenon he had to
account for in a long life. . . . So one-sided an education could have been
possible in no other country or time. (pp. 34, 35)

Yet, this new group was still insecure enough to feel threatened by
socially disruptive forces (the matter in need of controlling) prevalent
in the late 19th century—industrialization, immigration, and urbanization.

This discourse emphasized mass education as the central force to
propagate a particular segment of the American population's sense of
morality and cultural mission. Public schools were also to incorporate,
by force if necessary, all the so-called marginal folk: the mostly southern
European immigrants with somewhat different notions of what it meant
to participate in the American dream, and the recently freed slaves
attempting to enter mainstream society.

By looking at the beginnings of the institutionalization of common
schools, one begins to identify a certain Protestant theme: a wide-
spread belief and assumption, even a mass fantasy, traceable to the
colonial Puritan symbology of the errand into the wilderness. The
colonial Puritan symbol of the errand and its linguistic tools of preservation—the jeremiad (in its historical forms and as public sermon)
for the adults and public education as a means of moral inculcation for
the young—arose out of the Reformation belief that actions needed
to be given words and explanations and that no action or idea was
self-evident. Obviously, this belief arose out of the shift in theological
understandings during the Reformation, a time when Protestants decided that one had to find salvation on one's own through the reading
of the scripture and not rely on the Pope to deliver the message as a
mysterious missive from God. God could be experienced directly
through the reading of the Bible. This reading was a moral imperative,
and the act of obeying the imperative was considered education. From
the mid-to-late 19th century, a time of great hope and trepidation
about the future of America and its mission, purpose, and place in
world history, such a ritual occurred.

Social jeremiads spilled out from the pens of Emerson, Hawthorne,
Thoreau, and Melville. Educational jeremiads came from William Tor-
rey Harris and from the later Progressive era writers Ella Flagg Young,
John Dewey, and Jane Addams, to name just a few. No longer was Amer-

ica small enough to contain any illusion of cultural coherency, something even the Puritans lost after a century, if not before.

However, a cultural coherency was desired, and the loss of the artificial belief in a coherency was believed a threat to national identity as understood by mainstream, White America. Writer after writer knew how to start the process of preserving the errand: Begin with the very young, as the assumption was that children were the most malleable. This idea was given credibility by the emerging technological discourse, which was perceived to promise not only control over the individual and community at large, something the Puritans sought but whose language and interpretive processes made impossible, but also linguistic control over meaning. In other words, technological progress was infused with an almost sacred zeal and import, although the language employed to express these impulses functioned to actually limit the symbolic meaning. Clarification for all, not individual interpretation, and the identification of what sort of behavior was acceptable at all times became the process and object of the moral imperative (Stivers, 1994).

There was a faith that such a powerful and regulating discourse would solidify the new middle class's sense of being the new chosen by perpetuating a notion of culture into the future (i.e., children) and, therefore, operating to control any marginal or radicalized beliefs that could not be incorporated into the errand operation of hegemony. Again, anxiety, faith, and righteousness were wrapped together in one cultural symbol, like fibers of a rope. William Torrey Harris (1874), educational jeremiad writer and one of the most influential national voices of mass public schooling at the end of the 19th century, spoke gravely of the import of public education:

> [T]he school is obliged to lay more stress upon discipline and to make far more prominent the moral phase of education. It is obliged to train a pupil into habits of prompt obedience to his teachers and the practice of self-control in its various forms, in order that he may be prepared for a life wherein there is little police restraint on the part of constituted authorities. (p. 13)

Diversity in America and great social disruptions at the time made necessary, in the minds of the Anglo-Protestant urban middle class, a centralized location that each community could control and dictate its values to. Public schooling became a moral inculcator, the means by which the errand into the wilderness symbology would be disseminated, even as the public discourse moved away from explicit moral language to the implicit morality of the new technological discourse.

It was no longer necessary, in the mind of this new urban American Protestant middle class, to be explicit about what it meant to be an American or how an American should act because it believed it knew. The middle class looked into the mirror and saw America, that symbolic and imaginative legacy of the Puritans. The key for the Protestant middle class during this period was to identify, control, and convey cultural knowledge to the young in a way that hid their political agenda. Morality was embedded in this knowledge and, as such, the child no longer had to struggle with individual morality because school would tell him or her how to act as well as how to think about his or her identity in terms of self, community, and, most importantly, nation. In some ways this was an updated form of the Puritan belief in predestination. The colonial Puritans believed God had already determined whether an individual was to be a chosen one or not. The individual's charge, the individual's moral imperative, was to reveal whether or not he or she was chosen.

A secularized version of this moral imperative emerged and was translated into tracking those children who would and would not benefit most from the wealth and goods that society had to offer. The difference, of course, was that the child was not given an opportunity to find out for himself or herself, except in the most obvious, well-mapped ways. School would determine for the child. What historian Arthur Schlesinger, Jr. (1991a) declared about the present age speaks to this basic assumption of school as the key to national symbolic identity and American morality: "The debate about curriculum is a debate about what it means to be an American" (p. 17).

To become an individual in this sense was to become what was presented as the symbolic America. Socialization proceeded in the way in which a student became an individual but only after he or she became an American, which meant embodying all the moral characteristics believed necessary to preserve the national identity, the national errand as appropriated and interpreted by the urban Protestant middle class.

The language employed to express both fear and hope, to fill in the format of the jeremiad, began to shift as society moved from a wholly theological/ecclesiastical structure to one that developed into what many historians and sociologists call a civil/religious or a secular structure that embodied many of the Protestant religious assumptions (Tyack & Hansot, 1982; Wuthnow, 1989). In effect, the Anglo-Protestant middle class reduced moral questions to technological problems. To the Protestant middle-class American, especially after industrialization had altered the urban landscape in profound ways, technology was believed to be the solution to many of America's social and economic problems. There was no reason to expect that the technological discourse would not do the same for improving the moral behavior of students, with the expected result being a perfect America (Stivers, 1994).

The child was now to embody a predetermined sundry list of morals, which in turn would have a different effect on each child depending on that child's "cultural" history or future status. America, in terms of world power, grew exponentially over the century and, until recently, maintained a sense of identity in terms of its place in the world. That sense began to diminish during the 1960s, but has again risen to a near fever pitch at this turn of the new millennium.

EDUCATION'S FUNCTION

In 1883 an editorial writer for the *Philadelphia Press,* in the space of two sentences, expressed the general spirit of the Protestant American urban middle class. Education was reduced to public schools; and the cultural function of public schools was reduced to the construction and control of character in the belief that such moral direction would preserve the Protestant urban middle-class' sense of itself as *the* reflection of America: "The great end of education is not information, but personal vigor and character. What makes the practical man is not the well-informed man, but the alert, disciplined, self-commanded man" (quoted in Linn, 1883, p. 81).

Education of the young became education of the "practical" being. The practical being was moral, Protestant, and one who would submit to the general economic system by conforming his or her behavior to the needs of industry. He was also to be loyal, yet at the same time capable of aggressive pursuit of economic goals as a way to better provide for family, self, and society. A moral being understood contexts—moments when the different possible character attributes best came into play. In other words, he was competitive and boisterous when deemed necessary, silent and passive and punctual the rest of the time. She was capable of dealing with any domestic dilemma, although always in a calm and nurturing fashion.

The practical being understood his or her circumstance in a way that did not question his or her condition within society, much like Puritan leader John Winthrop intended. But the individual was not to question much else within himself or herself. In other words, humans were transformed into the matter, the content, that a certain general discourse or form would regulate. The Protestant urban middle class, for the most part, participated in this discourse by submitting to its governing structure. This practical being was celebrated by educators in a way that sought to reveal, to rediscover, and to celebrate the larger vision of America's historical significance in the great cosmic scheme. As one educational speaker at the 1889 National Education Association (NEA) conference proclaimed, formal education was to become the element linking all of American life and institutions together. In her speech, Dutton (1889) proclaimed:

> The school life, brief as it is, may reasonably be asked to furnish to the Republic loyal and obedient citizens; to the business world, men with a courage and a grip that will not too easily let go in the pushing affairs of trade; to the social life, an ease and grace of manners, a strength of self-reliance, which shall put each in possession of his full powers for his own up-building and for the advancement for his associates. (pp. 487–488)

Such words no longer arose out of a religious theology, although the religious impulse infused it with evangelical zeal. Instead, salvation by way of America was a social theology, and the institution of school was to be its church. Kaestle (1984) described this phenomenon: "When educators of the nineteenth century spoke of principles common to all religious denominations, they meant all Christian denominations, and when they said Christian, they meant Protestant" (p. 104).

These general principles, infused with a worldview passed on many generations, were expressed in schools, although not in religious language. In part, this was due to virulent conflicts over the subtle differences between theological doctrines and to the increased popularity of another discourse by those urban middle-class Protestant professionals participating in the development and maintenance of mass public schools, a discourse filled with technological and mechanical metaphors (Stivers, 1994). Bowers and Flinders (1990) labeled this pervasive discourse *technicist-rationalism*, which, during the late 1800s and early 1900s, was driven by the desire for bypassing cultural differences and for providing a step-by-step process (curriculum) of moving each student up the ladder to his or her expected social position; a mass production model. Bowers and Flinders (1990) wrote:

> Thinking of education as a process of technological production is clearly revealed in a conceptually limited metaphorical language: education as "management process," the student as "product," and behaviors as expressions of . . . "competencies," or "outcomes." This technicist pattern of thinking, with its machine-like analogues, . . . reflect[s] the masculine concern with rational control and power. The basic assumptions of this tradition that are absolutely essential for supporting the technicist orientation taken in the classroom management paradigm include (1) a view of the rational process as culturally neutral, (2) a view of language as a conduit, and (3) a view of learning as individually centered. (p. 9)

As Bowers and Flinders (1990) pointed out, those participating in the technicist-rationalist language were intensely concerned with the behavior of each child within the classroom. This discourse seemed to provide effective means by which to categorize, measure, and direct a child toward preferred goals, all the while claiming cultural neutrality.

In general, the effect of the appropriation of technicist-rationalist discourse supplied a new definition of education, and, therefore, a new purpose for common schools. The institution of mass schooling would now function to transmit cultural values—soberness, hard work, self-control, silence, punctuality, and competitiveness. These values were presented not as particular mores that emerged from a particular culture in a particular time, but as universal and cross-cultural. They were now self-evident, due to the belief that language was but a conduit and carried within it little need for interpretation. The teacher supplied interpretation. Education became how well a student received and retained the correct knowledge, not what the student did with that knowledge or how the knowledge transformed the student in some "spiritual" way.

In effect, Protestant America's offspring would now receive these "virtues" in a formalized way from schools, and schools, as such, began to assume a larger share of the child-rearing duties formerly charged to the family. But schools would also prepare the offspring to assume future leadership roles by playing on the inherent either/or structure of middle-class Protestant morality. In other words, the leaders would be the ones who best operated in each social context in a way that would secure their images as the "best and the brightest." A leader, a naturally superior American, the logic goes, intuitively presented to the world a Janus face. What this means is that he could, simultaneously, be interpreted as acting aggressively, harsh, self-serving, and loyal and at the same time compassionate and team-oriented.

These few, cultural elite, these "natural" leaders, were charged with expressing for the rest of America what was necessary for progress, for the preservation of the errand. In effect, the institutionalization of education seemed to provide a tenuous cure for the anxiety felt over the uncertain future, as well as a guarantee to further social aspirations of the various urban middle-class groups.

Curti (1959) demonstrated in his study of the social ideas of American educators how moral education was to function in this way:

> It was easier to formulate objectives than to work out concrete methods by which education was to perpetuate republican institutions. Almost without exception, however, educational writers pinned their faith to moral education as the means of affecting that end. . . . For most educational writers an important part of moral training was the inculcation in the schoolroom of respect for authority in order to prevent the anarchistic dissolution of republican society. . . . It was the contention that the maintenance of rigid discipline and authority in the schoolroom was by far the best means of inculcating respect for law and order. (pp. 59–60)

On a second front, public common schools would also equip the ever more organized professional urban middle class with a mass structure to control and reform the urban underclass. Such an institution would pull the children off the streets and out of the factories or away from "suspect" immigrant parents. Again, those with natural gifts, no matter what cultural environment they emerged from, would rise to the top, for they inherently embodied the correct cultural Protestant attitudes that had become naturalized as America's essence. However, the criteria by which the gifts were determined began and ended in an interpretive framework urban middle-class Anglo-Protestants could accept and with which they could define themselves (Bullough, 1974).

Bloom (1987) wrote in *Closing of the American Mind* of the expectations of immigrants and, in the process, illustrated the continuing power of the Puritan images of light, despite the privileging of a secular language, and of the need for education so that the immigrants, too, would experience enlightenment in the Protestant moral ways:

> The old view [Bloom's favored view] was that, by recognizing and accepting man's natural rights, men found a fundamental basis of unity and sameness. Class, race, religion, national origin or culture all disappear or become dim when bathed in the light of natural rights, which give men common interest and make them truly brothers. The immigrant had to put behind him the claims of the Old World in favor of a new and easily acquired education.... There was a tendency, if not a necessity, to homogenize nature itself. (p. 27)

If the immigrant families failed to follow the new compulsory education laws, another regulatory force entered the picture. City police were found to be effective in dealing with adult immigrants considered too old to "educate." Despite certain Enlightenment notions, tolerance during this era was not perceived as necessarily a good thing—indeed a Puritan inheritance. The compulsory laws did not appear overnight as a consensual element to the control and propagation of the errand symbolism. In fact, there was much tension over the fact that such compulsory laws would remove children from the workforce, children who before made enough money to help the family begin the rise into middle-class status. So, compulsory laws had the effect of also being exclusionary even while they incorporated all, through common school education, into the cultural habits necessary to perpetuate the errand.

This impulse to reform had the effect of pulling children away from their parents' zone of influence. A child was to be raised in the ways of the errand by the force of compulsory laws. Immigrant children, along with urban middle-class Protestant children, were to begin school early and remain there throughout the adolescent years. This, in part, was to satisfy the urban Protestant middle-class obsession over immigrant children entering directly into the workforce without "proper" moral training or, worse yet, taking to the streets unsupervised (Wiebe, 1967). Such conditions furnished the urban middle class with a rationalization to label immigrants and their children as immoral, uneducated, uncivilized (insane), and, as concrete evidence of the evil effects of urbanization, without the firm control of a guiding hand.

A dominant belief during this period was that only certain types of human behavior could undermine America's (urban Protestant middle class) errand into the wilderness, an errand to reform all that represented nature. It was not a difficult jump for many urban middle-class Protestants to associate the immigrants with the state of "nature" (and so childlike and immoral). This condition, as framed by the Puritan symbolic inheritance, also was identified as existing within each individual at birth, a condition to be transcended. This notion lent itself to the interpretation that immigrants were but wild children who could not achieve moral transcendence on their own. Immigrants were to embody the moral conventions of the urban middle class and be reformed.

The logic was that "man" followed the same clock-like, linear, and "natural" path as the rest of the cosmos. Therefore, children were born in a state of nature (nature as understood after the fall of Adam and Eve), meaning they were depraved, or, at best, a bundle of potential. Only through the process of each individual becoming "educated," a process of transcendence into adulthood and into a harmonious relationship with God and the institutions of American society, could the ultimate individual, America, complete its errand.

The nation was still an infant, a child, even though it embodied the next stage of historical progress. And a child needed a strong parental hand, moral direction, and codified purpose to better mature into a civilized adult. Such were the invocations of most post-Revolutionary thinkers of the late 18th and early 19th centuries. The infancy-to-adulthood metaphor, in relation to both new nation and new American child, was powerful and an extension of the Puritan process of perpetuating that moral errand, a process of education in which the child embodied the moral impulses of the American Christ/Adam—John Winthrop (Lewis, 1955). The implications were forever being boldly penned as warnings, in the same fashion as the Puritan jeremiads, of what could happen if moral action was not taken. An infant, left to its own devices, would collapse into savagery and lose his or her moral imperative, his or her role in history and God's overall plan of Progress (Kaestle, 1984). Simply, education of the young meant enlightenment and the lack of it meant darkness. Thomas Paine summed it up this way: "The mind once enlightened cannot again become dark" (quoted in Wood, 1992, p. 190). What one was being enlightened to was nothing less than the correct morality that suited the social condition, supporting the process of American maturation.

To transmit morality was to give immigrants and other poor a "fighting" chance, or better, to further a final acceptance of their "natural" place in society. These notions reflect the same intent John Winthrop had for America. While sailing across the Atlantic, Winthrop spoke what would become a deep assumption, a Puritan creed: Some were meant to have social status and wealth and some were not; that was the way of the world, the will of God. Winthrop told his errand mates that once in America God's Will would be no different.

If a child succeeded in school and actually rose to a status that seemed beyond his or her station, such behavior was deemed acceptable and illustrative of the elevating possibilities of formal schooling. Simultaneously, an expectation was that the "other" would realize that his or her natural place was to remain on the fringes of mainstream society. "Success" satisfied some of the threads of the discourse of individualism so celebrated by many professional businessmen, including self-reliance, hard work, and a competitive edge, which seemed in conflict with many of the moral attributes (obedience, silence, loyalty) so revered and perpetuated through the schools. Again, to rise above one's station was a moral attribute, as long as the effort included a submission to the constraints and vagaries of the greater cultural mission. However, the opportunities for such an ascent, when speaking in terms of the poor and of immigrants, were few.

Schooling was also presented as a way to help those not born into the ways of the errand to pull themselves out of their "lesser" moral nature. In 1900, this notion of uplifting the "weaker members of society" was to include not only the abstract moral principles of the Protestant culture but also the Puritan obsession with the body, for many immigrants were perceived as dirty. Immigrants became objects by which to differentiate desirable and undesirable attributes. Purity meant not only that of the soul but of the body. Cleanliness had now become a sign of the near perfection to which American civilization had risen. To achieve this health, to maintain such a perfect society, a "contemporary civil engineer advocated the introduction of 'rain baths' in the public schools" (White, 1969, p. 175).

Gerhard (1900), an engineer, wrote:

> It is only by educating our poorer classes in cleanliness in early life that we shall make them, as a whole, love it for its own sake, and hate dirt and those habits which tend to make man lower than the beasts of the earth—too often now arising from an acquaintance, an intermediate association, with dirt and dirty homes among the poor. (p. 40)

Beyond the simple constraints constituted by moral maxims, a child ready to enter into an occupation would pick from that job whatever else was necessary to maintain his or her "natural" position (Bullough, 1974; White, 1969). From its inception then, education as a mass institution was limited to a particularized moral function, one that concentrated on the character of a child, a character that best suited and could be controlled within the current historical context. As Bullough (1974) wrote:

> Identification of sources of urban problems, in schools or out, focused increasingly upon the failures of individual character rather than upon disjunctions emanating from the urban–industrial milieu. Similarly, remedies proposed for urban educational problems concentrated upon inculcating the values of self-sacrifice, duty, morality, patriotism, industry, and thrift rather than upon attacking specific dislocations underlying slums, poverty, underemployment, and crime in cities. (p. 84)

When formalized education is considered a panacea, the implication is not that the institution will spearhead any great amelioration of human suffering. For the most part, the panacea notion refers to public education's supposed ability to inculcate the correct morality into a child in a way that prepares that child to understand his or her role within a national teleology (Perkinson, 1991). This history, then, would reveal itself to the world, would unfold in a way that would solve or at least resolve any social questions. A person's social situation may not improve by this movement of history, but education, the thinking went, would certainly mold that person's mindset into a moral predisposition to accept and think about what was happening to him or her in the "correct" fashion.

This expresses in the most general way the solid shift of education as an activity of engaging in moral questions and culminating in the possibility of salvation to the preservation of secular conditions in a way that seeks to control human social behavior without concern for spiritual transformation.

Again and again in the *Journal of Education, Education,* and *Educational Review,* the most prominent educational journals of the era, one reads of the desire to condition children into a righteous respect for the law, for authority, for the present social atmosphere. In fact, the *Journal of Education,* between the years 1880 and 1890, published more than 150 articles explicitly discussing the moral function of schools. The conclusion was that while Progress may or may not improve the child's situation, the child would at least learn what his or her "natural" social place would be.

However, this did not minimize the number of jeremiads that poured out of educational journals and in public speeches by educators who sensed a great opportunity in schooling. Writer after writer offered poetic ruminations and exhortations, rationalizing such shifts in the meanings and role of education through the use of Puritan images. Mowry (1886) offered such images in his "Moral instruction in the public schools," given before the State Teachers' Association in Rhode Island and later published in the *Journal of Education:*

> The problem before the teachers is this: Given (1) the youth of a nation, fresh from the hand of nature and given (2) all the surroundings of these youth just as we find them—good, bad, and indifferent—(3) how shall we nurture them into true manhood and womanhood so as to produce the maximum of virtue, usefulness, and happiness, and the minimum of vice, crime, and misery? The next generation of this nation is to be just what mothers, and the teachers, the home, and the schools of today make it.
>
> Obedience to parents, obedience to law, truthfulness, honesty, honor, purity, benevolence, and obedience to conscience as a paramount duty— all these are to be taught in all schools, at all times, and in all ways. They are like the actin rays of the sun, intertwined in all arithmetic, reading, geography, history or botany.
>
> Good manners and good morals like the exhilarating rays of the balmy spring sunshine, expand the germs of all study, and cause the roses of chemistry to blossom among the green leaves of natural philosophy, and the wheat of pure truth in logic and mathematics to ripen above the choked brambles and briars of skepticism and falsehood. (p. 75)

From his assertion of the problem to his prescription, Mowry was wrapped up in the assumption that one began with character, with a moral posture of how to approach schooling.

This urban middle-class Anglo-Protestant faith in institutionalized education was ironic in regard to the issues of morality. For Puritans believed that the dilemmas of morality were unsolvable and would ultimately lead to the downfall of mankind. For the Puritan, moral questioning had no end. Nor could such morality ever be institutionalized in a mass and explicit way. Not only was moral questioning, the act of interpreting the symbols, for the most part an individual event, it also was shifting to whatever social conditions would arise to tempt the vigilant Puritan.

Despite these institutional and linguistic shifts, the moral imperative persevered, if foundationally shaky, even in the late 1800s and early 1900s. As Bird wrote in *Looking Forward* (1899):

> Each American must preserve his or her cultural identity by defining him or her self as a production and representative of the United States of America,—bounded on the north by the North Pole; on the South by the Antarctic Region; on the east by the first chapter of the Book of Genesis and on the west by *the Day of Judgment*. . . . The Supreme Ruler of the Universe . . . has marked out the line this nation must follow and our duty must be done. America is *destined* to become the *Light* of the world. (pp. 7–8, 234, emphasis added)

The process of embodying America remained, but it was quite a different experience due to the shift from the literal/figural language of the colonial Puritans to the simply literal, technically operative, and impositional language popularized during this era. Most children (i.e., immigrant and poor) were now expected not to question, for all the pertinent questions had been answered, or so it was believed, despite the inherent ambiguity in each proposed notion of morality. The simple maxims were believed to be all that a child would need. Many educators asserted that this imposition was necessary to "transform" the child into an adult, part of the symbolic process of embodying America, although the professional middle class shed the language that for the colonial Puritans had given the symbols flexibility and room for interpretation.

A useful way to explore with more depth the words and contradictions and struggles in defining the morality of the errand is to examine the life of William Torrey Harris, a celebrator of public education and of the urban Protestant middle class as rightful guardian of the errand symbolism. Harris provides a window into the transition between the colonial Puritan and the technicist-rationalist discourses in terms of what education came to mean for different populations, as well as how the process of engaging in the moral imperative translated into different meanings for different students. Harris was education's most prolific jeremiad writer. He placed within the institution of public, formalized education the future hope of the errand.

6

Public Education
as Moral Transcendence:
William Torrey Harris
and the Errand Impulse

[T]he school is obliged to lay more stress upon discipline and to make far more prominent the moral phase of education. It is obliged to train pupils into habits of prompt obedience to his teachers and the practice of self-control in its various forms, in order that he may be prepared for a life where-in there is little police-restraint on the part of constituted authorities.   —*Harris (1874)*

D URING THE LATE 1800s and early 1900s, a number of educational leaders emerged to articulate the impulse to school each American in conforming to the new middle-class perception of national identity. One of the most prominent voices was William Torrey Harris. Harris was a chief example of one who moved away from the theological jargon of his ancestors, the colonial Puritans, and toward the greater use of social science and philosophy as a means to continue America on its sacred/secular path of the errand into the wilderness. He produced a line of thought that was as determined as his colonial ancestors had been to clarify uncertainty. But in the end, as the colonial Puritans understood well, this line of thought generated as much ambivalence, hope, and fear, and fervent calls for schools to become the great savior of America's destiny.

Over the span of five decades, Harris wrote more than 500 articles (Lyons, 1964) about the design, meaning, and purpose of public education in America. He addressed the National Education Association more times than any one else in its history, founded and edited the first American philosophical journal, *Journal of Speculative Philosophy*, and served as editor-in-chief for several editions of *Webster's International Dictionary*. During his administrative career, Harris served as the superintendent for the St. Louis public schools as well as the U.S. Commissioner of Education (1889–1906). From this national pulpit, he delivered social and educational jeremiads—sermons that warned of the dangers of not embracing public school as the institution best suited to serve America's errand into the wilderness and preserve and perpetuate the morality of the Anglo-Protestant middle class.

Like most Protestant middle-class Americans who shared a New England Congregationalist cultural heritage produced by the colonial Puritans, the impulse to define education as an act of clarifying the moral complexity of life, and to see this individual effort as both crucial and a danger to America's destiny as a powerful light on the world, guided Harris' perception of how public school should function as a mass institution (Curti, 1959; Lyons, 1964). The institution was to be the means of transcending the individual into the institutional. Harris forwarded the middle-class belief that school was to instruct the child in how to surpass his or her animal, depraved self (a newborn's natural state) by embodying a greater identity, that of the American symbolic self, a self that escapes the vicissitudes of history and settles into an ideal identity produced by American institutions (Harris, 1885c, 1901, 1902).

However, the American symbolic self in the late 1800s and early 1900s multiplied in its meaning and effect, often in what appears a contradictory fashion. There remained the most privileged moral flight, that of transcending to Cotton Mather's symbolic construction of the first American, *Nehemias Americanus*, who possessed a body of virtues that all Puritans had to internalize to become "true" American individuals. However, the symbolic self had to adjust to incorporate a wider, more complex cultural system in a particular historical place and time marked by wide diversity of peoples. John Winthrop as *Nehemias Americanus*, the first American and a figural Christ/Adam, could serve well as a symbol for a small, unified, cultural group that perceived itself as chosen or elected to fulfill God's biblical scheme. The power of his moral appeal persisted and continued to symbolize the ultimate spiritual transcendence and national identity, that of America. However, no longer could the symbolic self of John Winthrop designate in a singular way an

American culture characterized by a diverse population spread out over a large geographical space. In other words, this particular process and object of transcendence (*Nehemias Americanus*) became unattainable for most Americans. Instead, a vicarious experience was substituted, that of transcendence to institutional servitude, which gave most Americans a sense of participating in the ultimate self.

What dominated the poor and afflicted and the great flow of immigrants was deference to and the embodiment of institutional morality, a morality represented by those who were given the actual opportunity for "authentic" individual transcendence. To buck the moral structure, the poor Protestant and émigré faced police action and jail. Such shifts in the possibilities of transcendence to a privileged national identity were no more evident than in the institution of education.

For Harris, the moral imperative for most students was to integrate with the American institutions by first submitting to a rudimentary morality as expressed by these forms:

> Each man is mostly a possibility, he has realized but little of what is in him. But when he looks out upon his community, upon his nation . . . through the window of history, he beholds his inner self reflected in a gigantic reality. He learns to know his greater selves—those selves that are too great in all-sided completeness to be realized in a single life, and which, therefore, take on reality through individual combination, thus forming the great institutions of the race. (Harris, 1885c, p. 449)

Harris articulated the professional middle-class sense of moral superiority and perception that some individuals were apt to rise above others and were chosen to regulate and direct the institutions. This followed the same mentality and thrust of the colonial Puritan conversion experience—once one experiences God's grace, he or she often assumes an elect status within the community and is given power. However, by the "normal" individual identifying with the American institutions, he or she is "saved the trouble of trying over again what has been found in error, and hence is also saved the pain which comes from it" (Harris, 1901, p. 255). In other words, to preserve the gift that was America, a symbol that Harris believed represented the highest form of civilization, schools must assume the role of imposing on, or evoking from, children the morals that dominated institutional life. In effect, this meant treating children as abstract categories to be processed, packaged, and placed in society as efficiently as possible.

However, schools also shouldered the responsibility of guiding certain "elect" students up the hierarchical ladder from mere obeisance to the existing moral order, a rung on which Harris anticipated most would be content, to that of the highest spiritual transcendence of American and, thus, world leader. For certain elite or "naturally superior" members of society, transcendence translated into an individualistic act, although one that preserved the coherence and power structure of the institution. These individuals would ascend in the social system to become literal and figural representations (e.g., Harris in education) of how the morality of institutions would be perceived. In other words, these Americans (White and urban, professional, middle-class, Anglo-Protestants) were to embody the morals of the institutions as they grew older. In effect, this activity as delineated by Harris would reward each with an opportunity to generate for the next generation the meanings of the moral symbolic structure of America. These would be the "authentic" Americans.

These fortunate few would represent all that was ideal in institutional life and would be awarded the opportunity to participate in and accumulate to the fullest all the fruits that an industrialized, modern society could offer—spiritual and material treasures that few could fathom. Schools were charged with controlling the moral process of both possible American types. How to delineate and reconcile these two possible moral forms was a problem for Harris during his entire career.

HIS CULTURAL CONNECTIONS
TO THE NEW ENGLAND WAY

Harris had a New England heritage that extended back to 1631. In that year, his English ancestors arrived on American soil, settling in Rhode Island. The Harris and Torrey families were members of the professional class and "included businessmen, doctors, ministers, and lawyers," as well as bankers and large-scale farmers (Lyons, 1964, p. 10). All were highly educated and pursued the "leisurely" or abstract studies.

In fact, Harris, in an article discussing his own education, spoke of how his religious and regional background affected his reading of certain classics. Acknowledging his Puritan Congregationalist roots, he wrote that he gravitated toward morality tales, such as Milton's *Paradise Lost*, "[which I] eagerly studied for its view of the world, Calvinist as I was by family and church education" (Harris, 1886, p. 559).

And, as most men in his family before, he set out to attend Yale. He stayed 2 years. Yale was entrenched in faculty psychology and "sought to discipline the faculties of reasoning, memory, and imagination" (Lyons, 1964, p. 13). Despite doing well in his studies, Harris later (1886) wrote that he was "full of dissatisfaction with its [Yale's] course of study, and impatient for the three moderns—modern science, modern literature, and modern history" (p. 560). Harris never fully rejected the assumptions behind faculty psychology, the prevailing theory of psychology that considered the mind a muscle and that certain subjects provided the mind with a better "exercise" than others. A strong, muscular mind, the theory goes, trained by the repetitive memorization of Latin and Greek, generated more acute, insightful, and useful ideas (for further explanation see Pinar, Reynolds, Slattery, & Taubman, 1995). However, Harris was interested in exploring other means to arrive at the nature of humanity. He believed that a wider variety of subject content within the curriculum would make the mind capable and more engaged with the knowledge of the world.

His exodus from Yale was an effect of this impatient urge to reveal the foundation of things, an inherited impulse to question and discover the correct universal morality that could with certainty guide a life in both spiritual and earthly matters. He headed west, taking part in what Lewis (1955) called the common journey of the young American male: Leave home, shed the past, and create a new, transcendent "self." Harris stopped in the booming midwestern town of St. Louis. He would later describe his arrival as the first step in the moral experience of becoming an American individual. It was a "clearing up which arrives when one breaks away from use and wont, throws off adherence to blind authority, and begins to think for himself" (Harris, 1887, p. 142). His narrative conveys the idea that the individual was to rise above blind obedience and discover the moral truths on his or her own, specifically through a self-reflexive reading and interpretation of cultural texts.

In St. Louis, after accepting a position to teach in the public schools, Harris became a member of the St. Louis Literary Society. It was with this group that Harris began to grapple with certain persistent issues in social life that had plagued those living after the Reformation, particularly for the New England Puritans attempting to inscribe a wilderness with their own interpretations. The problem: How to reconcile the tension between the sacred need of the individual to transcend and hear God's world directly, as opposed to the State's need for individuals to submit to institutional moral conventions for the sake of order and the preservation of certain cultural practices.

In Harris' intellectual exploration, two simultaneous forces were at play. He was engaging in the colonial Puritan moral imperative of working to reveal and transcend his own "self," and, therefore, to find his place within the American errand during the rise of the middle class. Second, as part of that engagement, Harris appropriated a formal philosophy to enable him to express this inherited impulse and to try to reconcile this tension. The philosophical concepts were those of Hegel, who wrote during the early 1800s. Hegel, arising out of German Enlightenment, found himself attempting to reconcile the Pietistic thread of the Enlightenment, which tended to "defend the individual, his convictions and his freely chosen community against the larger official structure of the state and church which commanded allegiance" (Taylor, 1975, p. 12) and which emphasized an individual's "spiritual" or personal experience of God with the thread of reason and institutions as the highest expressions of God (or Spirit) and to which the individual must submit his or her will. The German Enlightenment had a strong affect on Calvinists in general, the Puritans in particular (Taylor, 1975).

Most see Harris' Hegelianism directing his philosophy of schooling (see Lyons, 1964; Mosier, 1956). There is an alternative perspective, however. Harris, as a product of the New England moral imperative, appropriated the Hegelian philosophy because of its interest in the same issues that interested Harris, and because of its language, which provided him with a nontheological discourse by which to explore these issues and apply his findings to the institution of schooling (for a detailed discussion on the specifics of the historical connection between Puritanism and Hegel's thought, see Taylor [1975]). Hegel's notions of historical dialectics and of Spirit (philosopher's God; translated from German *Geist*—mind, intellect, ghost) as the ultimate cosmic force entering into history to achieve its teleological end gave Harris a theoretical construct to explain how American institutions represented Spirit's accumulations, its current historical condition, and possibly even its end point. Hegel's philosophy allowed Harris to rephrase in a nonreligious language, because of its decreasing popularity as a mode of cultural expression, what Winthrop and his followers already believed and expressed in figural/literal language that was geared toward religious metaphors: that individuals, even after experiencing God's grace, must operate within earthly institutions; that in the grand teleology of Spirit, the preservation of American institutions, as the most divine expression of Spirit's presence on earth, is imperative.

This Hegelian philosophical elevation of institutions came at a time in Harris' life when he had stopped teaching and entered administration, a career that often placed him in a rhetorical position of contradicting his individualist philosophy of throwing off the oppression of authority to find one's self. As a member of the bureaucratic hierarchy, Harris absorbed the power to impose upon others, on a mass scale, certain meanings, rules, and methods of operating, all with a coterie of underlying moral assumptions, all emerging from the popularized belief that such standardization translated into an efficient execution of preserving a large scale institution. Once Harris rose to such a position, he fully participated in the protection and conservation of the nascent institution. He presented a powerful voice and rationalization of public education as the location through which his view of cultural identity and national mission would be sustained. As Curti (1959) pointed out, Harris was labeled the "great conservator" for just such reasons.

In fact, Harris' administrative reports in St. Louis and as U.S. Commissioner of Education were disseminated as models for how educational institutions should be perceived, organized, ordered, directed, and controlled. The actual format of Harris' educational missives were often copied by administrators around the country struggling to develop and institutionalize a bureaucracy in local school systems so that mass public education could be brought to all children in a uniform manner (Byerly, 1946).

Within 12 years of arriving in St. Louis, Harris had been chosen as superintendent of the St. Louis schools, which provided him a podium not only to promote the public expenditure of funds for the growth of public schools, but also to advocate his philosophy of education as a moral imperative. His words expressed a growing sentiment in St. Louis as well as throughout the northeast and midwest. During his tenure as superintendent, the enrollment in St. Louis schools rose from 17,000 to 55,000, and the first system-wide public kindergarten was created (Blow, 1910; Harris, 1903). Harris pointed to this explosion in the numbers of children attending school as a sign that he was correct in assuming that schools should be the institution of national moral preservation. In effect, numbers and measurements for Harris, as for so many urban middle-class Protestants, became the prime indicator of the correctness of their moral certitude. If something could be measured, it could be understood, and if it could be understood, it could be controlled, and a morality could be imposed (Kliebard, 1992).

SIGNIFICANCE OF INSTITUTIONS

For Harris, the American institutions of family, education, civil society, state, and, finally, church (in that linear, hierarchical order) represented divine expressions and the essence of Progress.

He expended a large share of podium time and filled many educational and philosophical journals with writings that rationalized mass institutions, despite his own admission that the ill effects of institutional life visited many Americans in different ways. Harris maintained a supreme confidence that all such "minor" inconveniences would be alleviated as America reached its dialectical end point.

As a universal, rational force that by necessity injected itself into history to seek its fulfillment, a state of absoluteness and perfection, Spirit was to always progress forward and produce for mankind, the recipient of Spirit's intentions, a more complex, rich, and powerful form of civilization. According to Harris, the cultural rewards were worth the possible devastation of any particular peoples, for in the end all those living in America would reap in some form or fashion at least a modicum of the treasures of Progress. And any effects rendered by Progress (which he used interchangeably with the Hegelian term *Spirit*) were "natural," necessary, and, therefore, acceptable and even desirable.

Apparently this rationale made it possible for Harris to perceive American institutions as not burdened with the faults of European institutions. In this discourse, Europe was portrayed as decayed by the dark forces of ancient history and deficient in Spirit, a force that had left the Old World behind in its dialectical climb up the historical, hierarchical, ladder. Spirit had positioned America near the brink of the end of history. America was now poised to peer back over its shoulder at the ravaged historical landscape, as well as to look ahead at the ever-closer possibility of transcendence, which was translated as social Utopia.

Social problems existed because they should and resolved themselves as Spirit propelled itself forward by means of the dialectic, a logical formation of thought Harris appropriated from Hegel and applied to American national identity. In short, by way of the dialectic, one posits that a thesis naturally produces its antithesis. The two polar opposites come in contact, from which a greater synthesis emerges. In other words, the tension generates a new condition in which the two forces are incorporated into a more complex whole. Progress was to persistently transcend its current state as it sought its final dialectical operation, which to Harris would culminate in the perfection of American institutions. In time, these American institutions would multiply across the globe and absorb all people. Harris wrote in a blunt way to justify American imperialism as an expanded errand; not as a brute act of power but as a "loving" act of saving people from themselves and educating them in the ways of Western civilization so that they could reap the benefits of Spirit's grace in America (Harris, 1899). The stated intention was that Progress was inevitable, as long as people from other cultures were to accept and abide by this moral maxim. The process of bringing others into the Anglo-Protestant, urban, middle-class's sense of destiny was a great concern for Harris, as it was for his colonial ancestors, as incorrect ethical behavior could prevent Progress. Each individual must behave within the moral conventions. Immoral behavior to Harris meant any action or thought that imperiled American institutional life.

According to Harris, the institution of the state represented the highest material expression of Spirit. An individual could never transcend himself or herself and actively participate in the higher reasoning of Spirit without embodying the moral codes of American institutions (Mosier, 1956). The state's responsibility was to organize human interaction in a way that provided the opportunity for each citizen to experience freedom, another Puritan cultural legacy that Harris (1901) expressed in Hegelian language:

> The state possesses the highest amount of rationality and on this basis has the right to dictate ethical codes. This codification of ethical observance is the most important function of the state. . . . The state organizes the world of human passions and desires, of human arbitrariness and caprice, into a temple of justice wherein the fragmentary will of each individual is pieced out and complemented by the organic will of the whole community, and thus made to reflect the divine will. (p. 261)

Immoral behavior would frustrate, possibly even disable Progress (Spirit). To engage in transcendence, one must become a being able to function according to moral conventions produced by institutional leaders and the public discourses employed by them. Public schools were to transmit this "knowledge" (Harris, 1881, 1883a, 1883b, 1883c):

The student must come to realize that the state is an expression of his self as it ought to be. To identify with the state is to identify with freedom since the state is an expression of the highest form of freedom, that is, freedom realized in the institutional life of people. (1902, p. 237)

In turn, each individual had an errand to run—to participate fully and wholly in an effort to sustain these nascent institutions, which now included a certain outcome of industrialization: the American corporation. To affirm and operate within the industrialized institutions of American civilization was to experience freedom: "The growth of corporations is the wonder of this generation; they do what the individual could never do for himself, and yet needs to have done in order that he may gain freedom from the thralldom of nature" (Harris, 1883b, p. 465).

By embodying the morality of American institutions, a child was to actually be lifted from his or her bodily constraints. To internalize institutional codes and to participate was a moral imperative, as well as an educative act in which one adopted the social order in place of "mere animal caprice" (Harris, 1901, p. 282). In this desire to transcend the "state of nature" through rational thought and interpretation, Harris restated the Puritan impulse to master and control not only one's external environment, so that it may better serve Spirit's needs, but also the depraved nature within each individual. Harris embodied the Puritan intent of willful reform, as well as the Puritan maxim, form controls matter. The responsibility for schools in this process was made plain by Harris' (1881) definition of education, appropriated from Hegel, although it sounds like another Puritan maxim: Education is "[a] process through which the individual man becomes ethical. . . . An ethical man is one who participates in institutions" (p. 215).

Constraints as generated by the morality that emerged out of American institutional life were theorized as necessary conditions of freedom, not impingements (Lyons, 1964). Again, these constraints were to control the only means by which America could be threatened—individual immoral behavior (Harris, 1888a, 1888b).

In the act of transcending the bodily self and embodying the greater symbolic self, as constituted by the moral identity supplied by American institutions, one was to receive greater knowledge and power to control the world around one (Harris, 1885a, 1885b). Harris wrote, "With the knowledge of the nature and time and space . . . man goes forth to take possession of the world and to make things serve his thoughts" (1885c,

p. 447). In effect, freedom emerges out of control. To acquire this knowledge meant becoming competent in the kind of discourses believed most able to produce the kind of control desired.

The general sentiment, which Harris championed, was that for America to take the rightful possession of the material earth, science, more so than religion, was needed. Religion was a discourse that furnished an opaque view into the mystery and origins of life; one was to experience without really understanding. In effect, religion reminded human beings of their helplessness. Science unveiled and explained and attempted to direct the view and the experience. The discourse of science and its offshoots provided a means to act on the privileged notion of control.

The language previously privileged as the means by which God (Spirit, Progress) would be revealed was religious or theological in nature. However, for Harris and the urban middle-class, Anglo-Protestant population, such discourse no longer provided cultural clarity, especially in a pantheistic society. In part due to the great social transformations—industrialization, immigration, and urbanization, not to mention the Civil War—many urban professional middle-class Protestant-Americans sought security and protection against what was perceived as cultural fragmentation. The vision of the errand was fading. Harris accepted the condition that religion still spoke to the "highest" moral values and spiritual concerns. But it seemed to produce more ambiguity in terms of making sense of the unstable cultural condition so feared by Protestant America. Other discourses seemed to provide just the opposite—certainty and control, an extreme recovery, in some ways, of the Puritan maxim "form controls matter."

The Christian worldview was to sustain its power as a beginning source. Science, as explained in schools, was to be the new discourse by which to explain and help attain the spiritual transcendence. Despite Harris' call that all institutions should abide by constitutional separation, the overarching worldview directing each individual and institution was to be Christian:

> It follows from consideration that social culture in the form of the church and the school as independent institutions becomes possible only as the basis of the religious world view of Christianity; and that the perennial continuance of the world view of Christianity, through the special form of social culture which belongs to the Church is a necessary condition

presupposed by the forms of social culture instructed to the school. (Harris, 1905, p. 37)

Harris (1905) was adamant in his attempt to clarify such a position:

My theme proceeds from the insight to lay down the doctrine that the first social culture is religion and that religion is the foundation of social life in so far as that social life belongs to the history of civilizations. (p. 18)

At the core of every American institution was the seed of religious origins, as well as a mirror of the ultimate self. As American institutions epitomized the "gigantic self," the study of the self could be translated into the study and the embodiment of institutions. This indicates not the melding of mind and body into a whole, but the refinement of the mind to gain control over and to direct the body as an affirmation of the will of the greater symbolic self. According to Harris and other idealists during the late 19th century, transcendence was an act of freedom from the earthly chains of wants and desires. In effect, the development of civilization, as illustrated by the building of institutions, transformed into an act of freedom from nature, which Harris defined as a state of depravity and animality.

Harris wrote that because his age was one of mechanical invention and productive industry, the mind was to take precedence over the body, which was more useful for brute labor. Harris proposed that American society near the end of the 19th century was at a point in which bodily prowess should be less privileged than the mental aptness necessary to pick up industrial and mechanical skills (Harris, 1882, 1883a, 1883b, 1883c, 1885a). For this to happen, an individual had to first suppress the animal desires of the body. The mind, then, would not get bogged down in mundane biological concerns: "Mind—not the body—is the inventive power, the directive power that can manage and use machine to advantage. It is a mental, not physical skill . . . man can make no progress in the conquest of nature without mechanic invention" (Harris, 1883b, p. 462). And the conquest of nature, this errand into the wilderness, underscored the need for Americans to direct their minds (form) to control not only their own bodies (matter) but the bodies of those who might possibly place in risk such a first principle:

The more educated intelligence, the more invention. The more *conquest over nature* by inventions, the more aspiration in the mind of the individual. . . . Perpetual growth in knowledge and wisdom, in the realization of man, to be discontented with the real, is, ergo, the lesson of civilization. (Harris, 1883b, p. 462; emphasis added)

If schools failed to impose control, which included convincing students to consent to such measures, then America's symbol of the errand into the wilderness, of America as the final production of Spirit, would be at risk. Urban middle-class students would never transcend themselves. Immigrants and/or poor children perceived as "naturally" immoral would not be trained in the needs of American civilization and, therefore, would threaten the embodied meanings of the symbolic structure:

> Either educate your people in common schools or your labor will not compete with other nations whose peoples are educated up to the capacity of inventing and directing machinery. If you cannot compete with other peoples in the matter of the use of machinery, you must recede from the front rank of nations in every respect. (Harris, 1885c, p. 448)

Again, the institution of school seems to make all other forms of moral education possible, for it is public schools' role to sustain the framework of national identity as a symbol of all that is "best," all that is privileged as "good" in Western culture (Harris, 1889a, 1889b). As the thinking goes, without the school's imposition of morals on students at an early age, the other institutions would collapse due to the lack of a coherent, unified citizenship and/or workforce with a sense of American vision and mission:

> Whereas civilization develops, there develops the schools, as supplementary to the family, and propaeduetic to the State, the Church, and civil society. The more advanced a civilization, the greater the complexity of its forms and usages—the more extended the fabric of institutions; hence, too, the more important the school, as a special institution devoted wholly to the work of training the immature individual for taking part in those complex forms of life. (Harris, 1881, p. 216)

One of the issues educational authorities had to address was to identify the moral virtues as characterized by institutional life that children must embody. This early intervention was significant because a certain few elect children were to later assume their place as cultural, and thus moral, leaders and heads of American institutions. For all Americans, excluding the tribal peoples that existed on the continent before European colonialism, the stages of moral transcendence to the ultimate spiritual self, as represented by those leaders within American institutions, began with the family.

THE FAMILY AND THE MOTHER TONGUE

The contemporary moral philosophy placed the child in the bosom of the family. According to Harris and his contemporaries, the Northeastern, Anglo-Protestant, urban, middle-class family provided the norm. In this context, the child experienced little sense of himself or herself as something individual or separate, and incorporated the language, prejudices, habits, and behavior of the family as defined within the industrialized, division-of-labor framework so celebrated by Harris. He wrote that the family

> furnishes the human being with his bundle of habits, his forms of behavior toward his superiors and equals; his habit of personal cleanliness, of proper dress, of proper eating and drinking, and in short, of the general conduct of life. It gives the child the knowledge of his mother tongue. (1882, p. 2)

The transmission of the mother tongue, in terms of speech and the first steps of reading printed texts, was the true indicator of a family's success in participating in the preservation of a symbolic national identity (Lyons, 1964). Harris (1877) made a direct correlation between the power of language and how one came to understand his or her role in ethical life. Throughout his educational career, he emphasized a child's ability to read texts as the supreme test of a successful school. In a Puritan/Calvinist inheritance that settled into a basic assumption about life, to read is the "primary, indispensable condition for the participation in the higher world of ideal humanity" (Harris, 1885c, p. 449). If the child learned to read the "best" literature offered by each subject in school, the child's inner eye would open to the light of his or her culture (Harris, 1881, 1883b, 1885c).

In a colonial Puritan echo, Harris maintained that without general literacy, the American identity would be in peril because of the belief that only through reading could a child come in contact with all that was moral and ideal about Western culture. The act of reading was to inspire a child to transcend himself or herself and participate in the ideal treasures of the larger, symbolic self (Harris, 1885b). For Harris, reading to instruct one's life in the "correct" art of living was the most spiritual of acts, at least according to statistical and social science research that Harris (1881) was quick to provide as proof of his claims: "It is shown in detail that the illiterate portion of the population in each State and nation produces from four to fifteen times as many convicted criminals as an equal number of the population that can read and write" (p. 227).

Industrialization had taken its toll, producing what Harris called certain unfortunate effects, one of which was the fragmentation of the family. He believed that the family, despite its designation as a cardinal institution (supposedly more precious than public education), was fragile and failing in health because of the moral crisis experienced by the urban middle class. The influx of the "corrupted" morals of the immigrant families "ignorant" of the American vision compounded the moral confusion and presented a greater hazard to America's moral superiority and elect status in the educational and social commentaries of Harris and his contemporaries (Higham, 1984). Harris (1881, 1884, 1888a, 1888b) asserted that public education functioned to prop up the family by assuming much of the "educative" responsibility.

When Harris became U.S. Commissioner of Education, his jeremiadic tone intensified. He warned that Americans must embrace public education as the institution to transmit the mother tongue needed to inculcate children into the conventional morals and habits of thought previously delegated to the family. This appeal also applied to all middle-class families because in many ways, the urban middle class perceived itself as the builder, reformer, and dominant participant in public school systems.

In effect, urban middle-class Protestant families began to extend into schools and schools into families. An indication of the popularity of this phenomenon was the quick growth of kindergartens, an effort in St. Louis led by Harris and Susan Blow. They developed a system-wide rationale for sending children to school at an early age. A child at the age of 5 attending kindergarten was, much sooner than before, to engage in the first "formalized" steps of the moral imperative, beginning with separation. This placed the child in a kind of social gray area: more creature than individual, yet no longer just an extension of the family. The animal self, especially that of willfulness against authority, wielded the kind of biological persuasion that a child would surrender to unless properly trained by schools (Harris, 1871, 1876, 1901). School was to curb this activity and redirect the child's energies so that he or she could separate from the bodily self and begin the process of embodying the spiritual, or higher reasoning, self:

> Whatever gives to the mind a larger view increases individuality; whatever gives to the youth the power of self-control and of inhibiting his impulses and whims for the sake of combination with his fellows increases his higher order of individuality and makes him a more worthy citizen, and in doing these things the common school system performs its greatest function. (Harris, 1902, p. 237)

SCHOOLING TO INDIVIDUALITY: MECHANICAL AND SOCIAL VIRTUES

If a child was but a depraved creature, with the fund of civilized thought and behavior buried deep inside the mind and waiting to be exposed to the light of the child's eye, public school's first responsibility became the swift blunting of this animal caprice:

> By nature he [mankind] is totally depraved; that is, he is mere animal, and governed by animal impulses and desires, without ever rising to the ideas of reason.... Out of the savage state man ascends by making himself new natures, one above the other; he realizes his ideas in institutions, and finds in these ideal worlds his real home and his true nature. (Harris, 1871, pp. 4–5)

During this time, a child was to become aware of his or her capability to balk at an adult's command. Harris declared that all such exhibitions exist outside the categories constructed as rational and civilized. Harris asserted that school should function to "civilize" the child, and so charged the teacher with the job of obliterating in fast measure the student's penchant for "irrational" behavior. Only through an act of control could the child, in later life, possibly transcend to a more "reasoned" state in which acts occur according to the rationale and needs of a cultural institution.

However, one could not beat the beast out of the child. The child had to willingly engage in the act of self-control:

> The school that is strictly disciplined by harsh methods, corporal punishment and the like, may become poisonous to the higher virtues. But the school that is governed by laxity, neglecting industry, silence, and punctuality, is far more deadly in its effects on the character. The martinet system of discipline is moral in so far as it gives those habits of prompt combination with one's fellows, but it is better adapted to galley slaves and prison convicts than to children of the public schools. (Harris, 1889a, p. 30)

The teacher was to evoke an inborn or essentialized desire within the child to inhabit the behavioral boundaries supplied by the school. In effect, Harris was evoking a Puritan moral imperative: The individual was responsible not only for seeking conversion and individual transcendence, but also for learning how to operate in the material world in an ethical manner as determined by received moral conventions. Once the child mastered such rudimentary ethical behavior, he or she could then engage in an act of "true" moral transcendence—learning to read (Harris, 1881).

Harris (1881) called the virtues revolving around the overarching theme of self-control the *mechanical duties* that a child had to embody so that his or her "natural depravity" would not interrupt America's errand:

> [I]n a well-disciplined school the pupil is first taught to be regular and punctual; to be cleanly in person; polite to his fellows; obedient to his teachers; he is taught to be silent and industrious, attentive and critical in his mental habits. To sum up all these in one word, he is taught to subordinate his capricious will and inclinations to the reasonable conditions under which he may combine with his fellow men, and share in their labors. (p. 226)

The mechanical duties satisfied the criteria of an economic, state, and church system in terms of what each hierarchical structure needed to preserve its cultural power:

> [W]e believe that a child can easily learn the lesson of willing obedience to lawful authority. We would therefore place him upon the basis upon

which he must stand when he leaves our care; under such circumstances alone we can predict that those whose school record is good will make useful citizens. (Harris, 1883b, p. 465)

Children had to learn first and foremost how to obey authority and learn how to play "adult" games. If a child was not silent, then no learning took place. A child had to be silent to possibly begin memorizing the general social habits—how to sit, how to stand, how to speak, and how to take orders. Another self-evident moral trope for Harris was punctuality. When Harris could not persuade with philosophical rhetoric, he turned more and more to that of social science, which was emerging as the most popular method by which to "prove" one's point. Harris applied all the statistical knowledge of the day to make a double correspondence—tardiness with ill-behavior and poor performance in school, and punctuality with "moral" behavior and superb school performance. Also notable was the way Harris extended the training of the child, in terms of punctuality, to the child's home. The parents, too, would be transformed into more linear, time-oriented individuals, something that the growing manufacturing community complained that immigrant and poor workers lacked (thus diminishing profit):

The number of cases of tardiness has reached the ratio of 52 to 100 pupils enrolled during the year, a number unprecedented in the history of the schools of St. Louis, or it may be affirmed, in the history of the school system in any other large city in this country. It confirms my remarks last year, to the effect that efforts of our teachers in securing punctual habits are gradually but surely working a reform in the habits of the community. (Harris, 1876, p. 17)

For Harris, moral transcendence was a linear and hierarchical process with a beginning, middle, and end. The mechanical virtues were the point of departure: "These simple duties seem mechanical, and are often despised; but they underlie all higher ethics and make possible all great combinations" (Harris, 1889b, p. 131).

Control suited Harris' perception of exactly what American public education needed in order to develop into a mass organized system. Harris spoke directly to the needs of administrators struggling not only to institute the idea of schooling as a mandatory act in each local community, but also to sustain a hierarchy and division of labor within the school itself in the belief schools could be more easily controlled and directed for the "common good" (another favorite notion of the Puritans). For Harris the educational philosopher, the bureaucratic administrator, social philosopher, and voice for a unified culture protected by schools, control became the premium constituent within the moral imperative of the errand. Control for Harris was not a negative operation. Control had a positive function. To embody the rudiments of control would possibly produce good tidings to those less fortunate—the common laborer and the poor (Harris, 1881). If schools succeeded in teaching children self-control, then all that which threatened America's symbolic place as the self-and-God chosen light of the world would be alleviated (Harris, 1881). However, professional middle-class Protestant Americans had to be ever vigilant. Immigration headed Harris' list of menaces to the culture that was his America. At same time, he perceived the wave of immigration as part of the great dialectical function of Progress needed to further America's mission. In fact, he even pointed to a certain "valuable" effect of immigration—a greater labor pool necessary for America to build a global economic powerhouse essential to assume its rightful role as world exemplar.

Simply, Harris considered immigrants a necessary evil. In fact, schools were to take the lead in protecting against the immigrants "moral weakness." He warned against schooling such children in any superficial way and then hoping the "moral problems" of the immigrant families would dissipate on their own. Progress could not be blamed for moral problems; only individuals not operating "authentically" within cultural institutions could (Harris, 1881). Harris suggested that immigrants would not or could not educate themselves in the ways of "American" culture on their own. The state had to assume that responsibility. A practical tact of handling the "immorality" of the immigrants and the poor was to increase the size of common schools to accommodate the immigrant youth. This had the effect of removing from the immigrant child too much immigrant family influence and allowed the Protestant morality to be instilled quickly and deeply:

> [T]hese causes of weakening of morality in our time and country are causes that cannot be removed, and that it is useless to lament. . . . No moral training will be equal to the emergency unless it gives inner strength of character such as will enable youth to act right in novel situations. (Harris, 1884, p. 123)

At this point, the process of moral transcendence had the same effect for all diverse collections of students, which for Harris included not only the middle-class, poor, and immigrant groups, but also all the different races (Harris, 1881). In fact, if the child was able to master the morality of self-control as defined in terms of obedience, silence, and punctuality, he or she, while still in the domain of common school authority, would "progress" to the embodiment of what Harris called the *social virtues.* These were extensions of the mechanical duties: obedience not only to self but also to others in authority; honesty to all; and justice and respect for the law (Harris, 1883a, 1884). Such virtues moved one outside of himself or herself into the realm of social interaction.

Harris stressed that these virtues would provide all other institutions of America with respectful citizens and employees who understood and accepted their social and economic lot. In effect, the individual would no longer have to question the why or wherefore of institutional control. Students were just to accept the institution's reasoning and morality as a universal truth and necessity (Harris, 1883a, 1886). For Harris, the moral dilemmas that the colonial Puritans struggled with and could never fully answer were now answered.

Harris and his contemporaries expected all children to master these two levels of moral transcendence—mechanical and social. If a child's schooling ended at this point, American institutions would be without risk as long as the school was efficient in its method of imposing a morality. For Harris, efficiency translated into the standardization of curriculum and administrative control across the nation's mass public school systems.

Common schools, then, were moral at the core, despite the fact that morality, as an explicit topic of study or discussion, faded during the 1900s. By the early 20th century, every act, subject, and method of instruction, in part, operated from the cultural assumption that American education was about embodying the identity of national institutions. For most Americans, the task of education ended there. Morality would be introduced into the curriculum without the student ever contemplating moral issues.

However, this was not the end of the moral imperative for certain students. Only those who continued their efforts beyond the common school could possibly master the ultimate rationality—the spirituality—indispensable in the moral process of transcending the animal self to that of an "authentic" individual (Harris, 1902). Only then could a man (women during this era rarely moved past the common school) receive the complete "wisdom of the race" (Harris, 1902, p. 229), a gift that enabled one to engage in the final moral transcendence. However, the final stage of transcendence went beyond institutions and directly to the source. A whole different sense of freedom was established there.

Freedom for most of the American population (those who finished common school education) translated into duty or the right to assent to the demands and needs of the institutions. For the individual who was chosen to transcend to the spiritual realm, institutions possessed no power to construct bounds. It is this stage that Harris labeled *self-activity*, a term lifted from Hegel that expressed a sense of ultimate transcendence, which Harris applied to himself. However, this transcendence and freedom presented Harris with an irresolvable conflict: What if the institution and a "spiritual" individual came into conflict? Would that condition possibly threaten the whole of the symbolic structure of the errand?

PARADOX OF SELF-ACTIVITY

When Harris considered his own journey of moral transcendence, he felt that he had achieved its highest point at the age of 50, a time in his life when he was reaching his peak in the field of education and enjoying the fruits of his *self-activity* (Lyons, 1964). The last level of education, according to Harris, was the realization of freedom from the constraints of others and freedom to act in accordance with "world Spirit" as a "true" individual whose intellect and will work in concordance (Harris, 1883b, 1901). In effect, freedom for Harris meant different things for different people depending on an individual's circumstance within a given culture.

In article after article, Harris interpreted authentic participation with Spirit as operating within earthly institutions in a competent manner. And those like himself who achieved such rational existence were to ascend to roles of cultural leadership. One who was free was one who understood the constraints of the institutions and learned to function within them in a way that bore all the possible fruit for the individual, and that increased the amount of control the individual could exercise over an environment.

Even though Harris never stated that immigrants and the poor should not or could not proceed to such a moral level (for his educational and philosophical discourse extended in public to all children), in reality, only a few prominent students continued beyond common school to high school, and even fewer to college. These individuals, according to Harris (1905), were to become the "spiritual monitors" for the community at large. Such a level of education was all but out of the question for poor or immigrant children until well into the 20th century. Industrialization needed laborers and the immigrants fulfilled this need at very early ages. Harris' notion of self-activity failed to reach their ears or eyes except in the discussion of a particular kind of freedom—the freedom to assent to institutional moral convention, which could be defined as a situated freedom. Harris (1882) applied this type of freedom to the mass of Americans attending common schools. He placed the "higher order" of human freedom within the domain of high schools and universities. In other words, such language was inevitably aimed at a small but powerful cultural group of middle-class, professional Anglo-Protestants with a family history of ascending to academics beyond the elementary years and who were in the process assuming positions of power within American cultural institutions. These "men" proceeded along a path much different from most Americans during the late 1800s and early 1900s: They followed that of *Nehemias Americanus* and embodied an individualized "self" that would represent the institutional morality to be received without question or resistance by other, less fortunate, Americans.

These elect individuals did not perceive institutions as antagonistic to their individuality, but as a merger of one into the other. A student who progressed to that level of rationality, Harris (1901) wrote, was able to express his or her intellect and will as a combined force through the institution. In other words, to Harris, little distinction existed between those cultural elite individuals and the moral forms of the institutions. They were one and the same. However, any act by an individual who had achieved this moral superiority and ultimate freedom must, by definition, be moral and representative of the institution. And therein lay an irresolvable paradox for Harris.

If "moral freedom is the ability to choose those alternatives consistent with the needs of society" (Lyons, 1964, p. 80), then it was possible that this self-determined individual could choose the alternative of negation. Or he or she could interpret the meaning of the alternatives quite differently from others. The individual had the potential of acting in ways counter to convention. There was much room for radicalism by these cultural elite, who could threaten the moral integrity of the institutions as "conserved" by Harris through his efforts to propagate a system of mass public schooling. National institutions sustained viability only through an individual's willingness to obey their moral forms. And for public schools, in terms of national identity, Harris represented the moral form.

As such, he could not fathom that anyone reaching the same moral transcendence as himself, the same level of self-activity and self-determination, could interpret the gift of spiritual insight in a way that would endanger the very institution he spent his adult life trying to build and preserve. His assumption about moral insight emerged from his belief that through the philosophical study of the self, one could locate and identify all the universal truths of Spirit common to all "minds." One had to interpret the revelations of Spirit, but Harris had faith that anyone achieving insight would interpret in the same way and understand in the same way. He did not confront the ambiguity at the core of his thinking, the possibility that two individuals could follow rational trajectories of moral decision making and come to opposing conclusions, leaving them with an irresolvable antinomy. Harris' attempt to clarify actually had the effect of making his position more ambiguous: "[M]oral freedom was the ability to choose those alternatives that are consistent with the needs of the society" (Lyons, 1964, p. 80). Harris resumed his institutional stance in which institutions generated the alternatives, as well as the criteria, and, inevitably, the determination of which alternatives would be chosen. However, Harris again placed himself in the middle of a paradox when he also defined self-activity as the realization that one must be self-determined, which translated into a direct relationship with the actual form of Spirit and not just its symbolic structure or physical, earthly manifestations (Harris, 1901).

Inherent in Harris' notion of self-determination, which the colonial Puritans interpreted as the religious experience of personal salvation, was the possibility that the individual might be graced with a state of morality that went beyond the earthly institutions, a morality whispered by Spirit or by God "himself." After this experience, an individual, if possessing other cultural credentials necessary for legitimization, could claim morality as a guiding force, even though his or her interpretation opposed the other cultural elite individuals who accepted institutional life and led the moral way.

Neither Harris nor his contemporaries had an answer for this. It was a paradox that public schools could not solve. In fact, schools functioned to perpetuate the paradox by continuing the effort to serve different populations in different ways. At the same time, under the prodding of rhetoric by such national leaders as Harris, the moral imperative was placed in the domain of formal schooling for safekeeping.

Such was the paradox of Harris' life. He attempted to be an individual striking out to discover his "self." And in the process, he identified himself as the individual in education to not only preserve the institution as he perceived it, but also identified his "self" as that which characterized the institution of education that was to be embodied by all other Americans. This is indicated by the very quantity of moral sermons Harris presented at national education meetings and published in national education journals.

What Harris and others like him oversaw was the institutionalization of the perspective that the process of moral transcendence should be located in public schools, and that public schools had the responsibility to produce individuals who would not only engage in the moral imperative, but also produce, as a form of limited transcendence, willing servants to industrialization's cause. Underlying each possible identity as that which represented part of the corporate body was the errand into the wilderness—the moral imperative of transcending the self to the larger self, regardless of the way one defined the larger symbolic self.

The errand, as institutionalized by those middle-class professionals and cultural elite, pulsed strongly throughout the 20th century, even while existing for the most part as an implicit foundation of thought. However, a century has passed and another crisis has emerged. Again, jeremiads are filling radio and television waves, as well as the printed page, replete with warnings from every possible perspective in America. The echo in recent years has become stronger and clearer: America has lost its moral compass and its unified cultural identity because of the failure of public schools, and only through the reinvigoration of public education can America be saved again and the errand preserved.

The gift has been handed down.

This chapter is a heavily modified version of "Morality and Public Schools: The Specter of William Torrey Harris," by D. McKnight, 1999, Educational Foundations, 13(4), 29–46.

7

Moral Crisis of America and Its Schools: Return of the Jeremiad Ritual

When we say we will put America first, we mean also that our Judeo-Christian values are going to be preserved, and our Western heritage is going to be handed down to future generations, not dumped onto some landfill called multiculturalism.

—*Buchanan (1992, p. 21)*

ANOTHER CENTURY has passed and another social jeremiad ritual over concern for the "errand into the wilderness" has materialized. Again calls are out that America's destiny is threatened (starting well before September 11, 2001, the day of the infamous terrorist attacks). Again the media is filled with voices charging public schools with both the blame of America's moral failings and the responsibility to save America's future. The impulse is powerful even though the discourses employed to speak of America's "errand" often conflict and challenge each other. The current jeremiads go something like this: Present-day America is perceived as immersed in a moral crisis because of certain cultural conditions. National identity has fractured, resulting in a pervading sense of uncertainty and anxiety about the future. Public schools, as institutions charged with preserving the symbols of national identity and a morality that is the concrete expression of those symbols, have failed and must be reformed. Finally, only through "schooling" can America be saved from this current cultural crisis. This is nothing less than what Hofstadter

(1962) cited as an "educational jeremiad," as "much a feature of our literature as the Jeremiad in the Puritan sermons" (p. 301). Zuckerman (1988) recognized the unease in the middle-class psyche: "And since our sense of history as always hinged on our heady assurance of bigger and better things to come, we now find ourselves adrift on uncertain seas, doubting divine direction of our mysterious voyage" (p. 13). The terms "mysterious voyage" and "divine direction" indicate an attempt by Zuckerman to evoke an emotional response. He is firmly within the lineage of Puritan historical and jeremiad writing. He laments this sense of a vision or metanarrative gone awry. For Zuckerman, the thicket of the dark wilderness is winning the moral battle.

As previous rituals have clarified, resolving the crisis is dependent upon schools remembering and transmitting middle-class cultural identity, and of the individual embodying the great institutions. Most of the current jeremiads describe in detail public schools' failure in this charge. Yet, at the same time, these jeremiads perpetuate public school as the institution most suitable to satisfy these national needs. According to the modern jeremiads, schools, and specifically teachers, no longer direct children through the process of moral transcendence—a state in which each child comes to understand and accept his or her role in society and fulfills this prescribed destiny in a carefully measured manner.

THE STORY OF AMERICA UNRAVELS

And though I can only look up and at a very steep angle, to Washington and Lincoln, let me remind you of their concern for the sometimes delicate unity of the people. The notion that we are and should be one people rather than 'peoples' of the United States seems so self-evident and obvious that it is hard for me to imagine that I must defend it. (Dole, 1996, p. 2)

Something of a mantra has emerged in public jeremiads over the perception of a modern moral crisis in and about America. The American story has fragmented. The once seamless plot of America as a country elected by a touch of divine grace and given the errand of sacred/secular progress has lost its narrator. A fear is that the deep celebratory voice has multiplied into many voices, mostly shrill, each with its own interest and story line. The complaint is that the national textbook has lost a cohesive symbolic structure by which to maintain the linear nature of the story.

Certain groups in America are scrambling to erase these seemingly "tangential" chapters and return to the central theme of an elect nation moving forward as long as its citizens stay true to the moral path. Nash (1993) indicated a deep-seated impulse to control and create a narrative coherence, which is part of the Puritan cultural gift handed down through the ages:

> Of course, the old coherence of the old overarching themes were those derived from studying mostly the experience of only one group of people in American society or in grounding all the mega historical constructs in the Western experience.... By showing that different groups experience a particular era of movement in starkly different ways, such terms as "The Jacksonian Age of the Common Man," "The Westward Movement," or the post-1945 years as the "Affluent Society," becomes only tall-tale labels of narrowly conceived history. (pp. 254, 256)

An eloquent partisan of the American story as clear, progressive and unified, even as its constituents are diverse, is historian Arthur Schlesinger, Jr. In the early 1990s, Schlesinger was a member of a multicultural commission whose charge was to rewrite the New York State curriculum in an effort to take into greater account the diverse populations of the state. Schlesinger was troubled by the path of the commission, which he believed sought to broaden the scope of history taught in schools to the point of disrupting any notion that America has had an identity, a history worth celebrating. He protested that America, as a single narrative generated from the symbolic impulse toward the "errand into the wilderness," was transformed by the commission into a cacophony of voices, each singing its own historical story without concern for how the piece works as a whole (Schlesinger, 1991b). Schlesinger (1991a) penned a polemic against the commission's decisions called *The Disuniting of America,* with excerpts published as an article the same year.

Schlesinger argued that although diversity is a fact of American life, a national identity with a common history still generates a means to manufacture and transmit the symbolic narrative and its moral constituents to children. Schlesinger (1991a) claimed the only effect of diversity would be violence:

> What happens when people of different ethnic origins, speaking different languages and professing different religions, settle in the same geograph-

ical locality and live under the same political sovereignty? Unless a common purpose binds them together, tribal hostilities will drive them apart. ... They [immigrant Europeans] expected to become *Americans*. ... They saw America as a transforming nation, banishing dismal memories and developing a unique national character based on common political ideals and shared experience. The point of America was not to preserve old culture, but to forge a new *American* culture. (pp. 10, 13)

Schlesinger asserted that those who wrap themselves in the multicultural label are ravaging the national identity of America even as they claim to merely be redressing past sins and including forgotten voices:

Unfortunately a cult of ethnicity has arisen both among non-Anglo whites and among non-white minorities to denounce the idea of a melting pot, to challenge the concept of "one people" and to protect, promote and perpetuate separate ethnic and racial communities. ... Its [ethnic gospel] is that America is not a nation of individuals at all but a nation of groups, that ethnicity is the defining experience for most Americans and that ethnic ties are permanent and indelible and that division into ethnic communities establishes the basic structure of American society and the basic meaning of American history. ... Multi-ethnic dogma abandons historic purpose. ... It belittles unum and glorifies pluribus. (pp. 15–16)

Schlesinger indicted the multicultural commission with attempting to change and control the future meaning of America by rewriting history curriculum in terms of ethnic groups and not as one people with a common vision and mission. Schlesinger (1991a) admitted that the notion of an American synthesis inherently has an Anglo-Saxon cast to it, but such a story is not an act of Anglo-Saxon domination:

The republic embodies ideals that transcend ethnic, religious, and political lines. It is an experiment reasonably successful for a while, in creating the common identity for people of diverse races, religions, language, and cultures. But the experiment can continue only so long as Americans continue to believe in its goal. If the republic now turns away from Washington's old goal of one people, what is its future?—disintegration of the national community, apartheid, Balkanization, tribalization? (p. 118)

Schlesinger did not dispute the necessity to rewrite the social studies curriculum into something more inclusive, but he believed that for the "book of America" to be successful, individuals must conform to an epic narrative structure dependent on easily identifiable characters. However, he appeared not to recognize that certain aspects of the discourse employed by many advocates of multiculturalism defend many of the same grand desires. Much of the mainstream multicultural discourse revolves around acknowledging ethnic differences, with the hope that toleration and understanding will actually lead to cooperation and a better social future for all (McCarthy, 1994); Schlesinger failed to appreciate the similarities between himself and them. Both reside within the same inherited symbolic framework.

Multiculturalists still attempt to preserve this symbol called America: They still believe it has a mission; a utopia to one day be realized. They still assume, or better, have faith, that school is the site to perform this service. Willie (1992) wrote that mainstream multiculturalism is concerned with saving America and Americans, not destroying it:

> [Multiculturalism seeks to bring] together individuals and groups with different histories and customs so they may mutually enhance each other . . . [and that] institutions are obligated to seek new members who are unlike those present. They do this not because it is nice to do so, but because diversity is essential to their creativity and problem solving. It is necessary for their world—and their survival. (p. 71)

An issue for those occupying the space of the multicultural discourse is that a single powerful cultural group—White, male, middle class—has distorted and corrupted America's origins and ideals, which should be revealed and written into the curriculum. Banks (1988), noted for his work in education and multiculturalism, claimed a national identity must still exist, an American identity formed not from just one dominant cultural cluster but from all cultures that call the terrain within America's boundaries home:

> National identification and related citizenship competencies are important for all citizens, regardless of their ethnic group membership and ethnic affiliations. National identification should be acknowledged and promoted in all educational programs related to ethnicity and education.
>
> However, individuals can have a wide range of cultural and linguistic traits and characteristics and still be reflective and effective citizens of their nation-states. . . . Individuals can have ethnic allegiances and char-

acteristics and yet endorse overarching and shared national values and ideals as long as their ethnic values and behaviors do not violate or contradict democratic values and ideals. (pp. 44–45)

Banks was explicit about an effect of multiculturalism. Even as it identifies and "respects" differences, what often occurs is a recognition of similarities on which communication can be grounded: "However, sociologically they [the different American ethnic groups] have many of the same traits and characteristics of other ethnic groups, such as a sense of peoplehood, unique behavioral values and norms, and unique ways of perceiving the world " (Banks, 1988, p. 45).

But the implication is that a lack of moral and ethical behavior by some has caused America to suffer and stray from its original intent of a more perfect society. For many multiculturalists, such a society should be measured and defined by its rhetoric of justice, freedom, tolerance, and the social "good" (Banks, 1988; Willie, 1992). In other words, the symbolic rhetoric extends to all those who call themselves American and who are willing to embody its democratic institutions and ways.

Again, moral behavior is crucial for the symbol to sustain authenticity. No matter which side one takes, a common consensus is that America has fallen into a dangerous, iniquitous moral dilemma. Moral vision has been lost. Schlesinger and others who participate in this discourse believe the truth and power of American symbols lay in transmitting to the young the notion of unum and blindness to ethnic distinction. Those participating in a multicultural perspective, in effect, put their faith in the future of America in pluribus, in the recognition of ethnicities as long as those ethnicities do not engage in disposing of the overarching national identity, which is necessary for a democratic society to function. From the perspective of both positions, the story of America does not deserve to be erased from what little American memory exists, the perception is that without historical understanding, America will fail to survive its "dark" moment, its modern moral crisis.

THE LIGHT DIMS: AMERICA IN A DARK TIME

And yet the genius of the American people is being stifled. Our economy is growing at the slowest pace of recovery of any period in the century.

Income of the workingmen and women in America is dropping or stag-
nant. There's kind of a gnawing feeling throughout the nation that in
some way, for some reason, there's just something wrong. (Kemp, 1996,
p. 3)

In late 1995 at a small Missouri university, sociologist Robert Bellah,
author of *Habits of the Heart* (1985), delivered a modern day jeremiad
to rival any given by Puritan clergy Cotton Mather or Jonathan Edwards.
Bellah distilled the whole of his assumptions about the current state of
modern American life down to seven words that served as a title for his
talk: "The Moral Crisis in American Public Life." The issue for Bellah
in his speech was not whether a moral crisis actually existed. Instead
Bellah's dilemma was to determine what constitutes the current crisis,
what are its effects, and what can rectify it.

In true jeremiad tradition, Bellah's (1995) proposals hinged on the
recovery of a Puritan gift forgotten somewhere along the national
ascending trail. His jeremiad began with a series of questions, each a
rhetorical satellite orbiting a moral center point: "How ought we live
together? In seeking an answer to this question, can society exclude
moral truth and moral reasoning? Can the biblical wisdom which played
such a formative part in the very founding of your country be excluded
from that debate? Would not doing so mean that America's founding
documents no longer have any meaning, but are only the formal dress-
ing of changing opinion?" (p. 1). Bellah (1995) seized on the logic that
places "freedom" within a particular moral structure, a deep-seated
colonial Puritan disposition, which situated him within the rhetorical
trajectory that demands a return to and retrieval of an "original" Puritan
intent concerning freedom:

Surely it is important for America that the moral truths, which made freedom possible, should be passed on to each new generation. Every generation of Americans needs to know that freedom—freedom that consists
not in doing what we like, but in having the right to do what we ought.
That startling idea . . . takes us right back to the very beginning of the
American project.

John Winthrop, first governor of the Massachusetts Bay Colony, said
something very similar in the seventeenth century. Winthrop distinguished between "*natural liberty*," that is the liberty to do what you list,
we would say to do what you want, and true liberty, what he called "moral

freedom in reference to the covenant between God and man"—which is a liberty "to do only which is good, just and honest." (pp. 1–2)

Bellah diagnosed Americans as addicted to "natural" freedom. He described a litany of moral failures due to Americans' embrace of the depraved and self-absorbed sense of freedom and morality. He asserted that this darkening is the worst kind of disease, for it begins with American leaders, the very ones who should exemplify the highest moral transcendence to individuality. This is a dilemma that even William Torrey Harris's moral remedies could not resolve. Harris could not deny that such moral transcendence also has the possible effect of an individual dismissing any other moral authorities except for him or her self. Bellah recognized this effect. He believed that one's acts may prove to run counter to the moral conventions of the day and threaten the very institutions that they were chosen to guard and lead. Bellah's list of national exemplars whose lives provided each American with a moral map to transcendence included John Winthrop, Abraham Lincoln, and Franklin Roosevelt. For Bellah, these men embodied the highest form of what it meant to be American. However, in the fire below he placed modern politicians, whose glib remarks glide without resistance through surface expressions of morality. He gave the example of an Associated Press story on former Louisiana governor Buddy Roemer. Bellah quoted the article: "Although Roemer was a moderate on social programs while in office, he has turned hard to the right and is now pushing for a return to chain gangs in Louisiana and backing much of [David] Duke's '91 platform" (quoted in Bellah, 1995, p. 2). Roemer responded in the article that he was only doing what the people wanted. Bellah charged that Roemer illustrates the lack of any moral compass in American leaders, each willing to shift with the prevailing winds of mood or opinion, each willing to be carried along rather than face the surge head on and risk ridicule.

Bellah's (1995) jeremiad contended an absence of leadership has exposed a darkness lodged deep within the soul of each American that may now crawl out unimpeded. Race relations remain tense. Immigration again is a serious issue. And the gap between poor and wealthy grows wider each year: "The shrinking middle class [has become] increasingly anxious about its future" (p. 3); the powerful and wealthy "overclass" (p. 4) has forsaken the "social covenant" in favor of increasing "natural" freedoms. This overclass encourages the mainstream middle class to follow its example. In this discourse, the set of freedoms translate into the demand to pay less or no taxes, to sheer away government regulation, and to reduce government itself except in areas such as military armament and crime prevention. The military is imperative because the wealthy benefit economically from America's intrusions into other countries to control the market economy. Crime is an issue because more money to "fight" crime equates into more police protection from the poor, with the effect of diverting attention away from the immorality of those with wealth (Bellah, 1995).

Bellah asserted that the discourse of the wealthy, designed to alleviate an anxiety or guilt over any act that might oppress another human, systematically constructs a social paradigm in which the poor have no one to blame but themselves. The middle class responds with ambivalence and finds itself hampered by a difficult either/or: Follow the lead of the rich in the expansion of natural freedoms, forsaking the inherited middle-class moral structure and its spiritual cast at the possible cost of losing a coherent national identity; or return to the project of "what they ought," to preserve the moral symbolism defined by the impulse in order to spread its social gospel to all and sustain clear, if not exhausted, national boundaries. The tension between the two does not function to paralyze the middle class, but instead develops a pendulum motion in which most Americans swing back and forth between having faith in the discourse of self-reliance and self-control and having faith in the discourse of community control.

Embedded in the psyche of the American middle class is a tendency to engage in a colonial Puritan discourse of individual moral conversion and transcendence. During the late 1800s and early 1900s, this discourse gave rise to the notion of an autonomous, rugged individual responsible for "his" own well-being and actions. This translated into the maxim that if one works hard enough and grounds one's actions in strong moral principles, then one will achieve the American dream, usually represented as being "right with God," the concrete signs of which include money, home, family, and security against the world's vicissitudes.

The impoverished represent everything that the middle class fear and desire to escape. For members of the middle class, who have experienced a real drop in net income and a perceived loss of spiritual purpose, the poor provide a means by which to define themselves. Uneasiness resonates in the recognition of just how close many middle-class families find themselves to a precarious financial position, closer to the realities of economic poverty than most like to admit.

Such signs became ends in themselves and not signs of something far greater in spiritual terms (Bercovitch, 1993; Stivers, 1994; Zuckerman, 1988). In the present age, such material rewards seem out of reach for many American middle-class families. This economic reality produces a pressing anxiety that America itself is under siege; that as guardians, the middle class has failed in its task of creating individuals who exercise self-control in favor of greater institutional rewards later. Self-reliance, however, still reverberates through the thoughts and actions of members of the American middle class, many of whom cling to the notion that one need only engage in hard work to raise himself or herself up to such a position in the world.

In some ways, the notion of mass public schools became a way of reconciling the individual self with social imposition. Schools would encourage the development of an individual able to rely on himself or her self, but the extremes that emerge when one concentrates solely on one's own wants would be tempered by the imposition of a moral structure with which the middle class as a whole could comply. Again, if one just learned to embody the moral errand, defined in the late 19th century by the middle class and institutionalized in the schools in terms of self-control at a young age, then the extremes of depravity brought by massive wealth or lowly poverty would be alleviated. Individual calls to return to the original American morality will inevitably fail, according to Bellah (1995), whose jeremiadic discourse exemplified the general middle-class sense of moral crisis: "As long as we are divided into overclass, underclass and anxious class most of us live under the threat of homelessness and despair. The other condition is that we repair our civic culture and strengthen our . . . national and global identities" (p. 9).

A predominant reaction to ritualized jeremiads such as Bellah's is the call to reform public schools. Instead of calling for a complete end to schooling, the response is to repeat a century-old rhetorical motion: Return to a time when schools "worked" and America was certain of its identity. However, in the present day, few can agree on what discourse is best suited to proceed with this nostalgic inclination. Many groups compete for the right to impose their language and meanings to describe and shape school reform. Some argue for a return to a "traditional" school curriculum, with emphasis on competition, efficiency, academic excellence, back-to-basics, and national standards. In effect, these traditionalists seek an institution that dispatches cultural knowledge in a way that can be measured against other societies (although they would claim the knowledge being transmitted is culturally neutral and so applicable to all).

BACK TO THE BASICS

And in no arena is an . . . overriding national identity more crucial than in our system of education. . . . Our public schools in particular have been the great instrument of assimilation and the great means of forming an American identity. (Schlesinger, Jr., 1991a, p. 17)

For the "conservative" wing of American culture, the crux of the present condition is that the institution of school has forsaken its "traditional" role of transmitting a basic core fund of cultural (presented as empirical) knowledge. Bennett (1992), Bloom (1987), Finn (1991), Hirsch (1987), and Ravitch (1985), to name but a few, developed such jeremiadic critiques.

Inherent in each polemic is a "back-to-basics" or "back-to-the-canon" mentality lauded by many national educational groups concerned that America's "center" (i.e., mainstream middle class that supports public education) has become morally corrupted by external cultural influences. The "center" needs reminding, so to speak, of the moral imperative involved in living "right," which translates into living a particular type of American life. The sentiment of this tight-knit, conservative cluster is that American schools have lost a vision and have become fragmented and diffused in an effort to respect and respond to every minority interest (not very different from Schlesinger, Jr., who has worn the label of liberal with pride). According to this discourse, schools must step outside of cultural politics and retrench to a system of political neutrality. This is supposed to constitute a nonpartisan stance that carefully delineates and dictates all subject boundaries, space, and time in a measurable way with clear, concise, direct language as derived from empirical science techniques. Indicated here are major assumptions, all connected, and all dating to the 19th century when schooling was institutionalized and the scientific discourse was appropriated by mainstream America. Among these assumptions: that knowledge could be directly dispatched through language; that knowledge was culturally neutral; that knowledge could be employed to control the environment.

The notion of cultural neutrality is ironic, particularly due to the expectations of the effects knowledge will have on each student. Those participating in this "traditionalist" discourse assume that each student will internalize a morality upon the transmission of knowledge, even though knowledge is supposedly without moral constituents. American values, according to this discourse, are natural and self-evident (and, therefore, categorized as universal knowledge). Simply, America (mainstream middle class) is knowledge. Students are expected, if given the "correct" information in the most "efficient" manner, to transform into skilled economic producers and "virtuous" citizens participating in a social system presented as representing the "good" and the "just." In effect, students will embody these values as long as they are imparted the "right" kind of knowledge in the most efficient, direct, and clearest way possible. In some ways, these privileged notions of directness, clarity, and efficiency function within the old Puritan metaphor of light, and the desire by the traditionalists is that public school must keep the flame—an American identity dependent on global military and economic strength and moral authority—well lit. Light will prevail as long as schools impart a coherent national identity in the form of a carefully controlled and measurable curriculum.

For instance, Hartoonian, in his 1996 presidential address to the National Council of Social Studies, stated that the Republic is under siege, that only moral discretion as determined by educational leaders and administrators will bring America back from the brink of destruction. The words are filled with a theatrical, almost melodramatic, flair for crisis thinking.

To spare American children from certain future disaster (the loss of a national identity in terms of world power and economic status tinged with a spiritual residue), educational leaders must peel away the "fat" in the curriculum. Hartoonian retrenched in nostalgia, believing schools must again produce students with skills to compete in a global market. Again, one can recognize a tension-filled juxtaposition of technicist language and methods with the impulse to give America a spiritual cast; a teleological purpose. "What Matters Most" (1996), a publication by the National Commission on Teaching and America's Future, performed a service for the "traditionalists." It supported nostalgic pleas (in the guise of moving forward in time) and technocratic assumptions within the mainstream duty of schooling.

The book-length report warned that without "basic" skills taught in schools, one cannot achieve economic success or join in the effort to perpetuate a "good" society. The faith is that in a "good" society, if an individual does not progress up the economic ladder and add to the wealth of a nation, then this individual cannot be happy. The report reminded Americans that they have forgotten how to be happy in their pursuit of property because they are not receiving the tools necessary to engage in this moral imperative, this material hunt, that promises America's continuing greatness on the world stage. The report repeated the process of trivializing and restricting the process of education. Education becomes but a form of schooling. According to this report, a direct correlation exists between the economic health of a nation and schools:

> Today's society has little room for those who cannot read, write, and compute proficiently. . . . The economy of high-wage jobs for low-skilled workers is fast disappearing. In contrast to only 20 years ago, individuals who do not succeed in school have little chance of finding a job or contributing to society—and societies that do not succeed at education have little chance of success in a global economy. . . . Business leaders announced their commitment to support employees' involvement in their children's education, to require evidence of academic achievement for hiring, and to make states' education standards a key factor in business location. (p. 3)

A shared stated intention is the need for a more efficient transmission of the basic skills of reading, writing, and arithmetic. Attached to this academic core curriculum is a form of "good citizenship" for the lower grades (social studies in the secondary grades) that places at its center a middle-class moral proviso that all children should be taught to value hard work, loyalty to God and country (which translates as one and the same), a nuclear family, church on Sunday, and economic security through merit. The belief is that if schools develop high standards as determined by national test measurements, spend more time imparting a "basic" curriculum, and construct better and more instrumentally attainable outcomes to better hold teachers and students accountable (and so sorted out [Spring, 1989]), then the symbolic structure as understood by the American middle class will be sheltered.

Simple "self-evident" maxims spoken to young children, and dressed in more sophisticated language for older students, mostly in the form of governmental studies, function as all the explicit moral training necessary. In the discourse of "back-to-basics" or "academic excellence" (both presumed to have existed in some prior era), the concept of education has narrow boundaries of meaning due to the language used to express it. In this discourse, the student is but an empty receptacle waiting for knowledge to be imparted. The student is to recognize the self-evident moral imperative embedded within that cultural knowledge, and the student must accept that education takes place, for the most part, in a classroom. The recent national reform thrust toward accountability and standards, well represented in educational circles by the National Commission of Accreditation of Teacher Education (NCATE) and President George Bush's education reform package that ties a large supply of federal money to standardized test scores, has refined this schooling impulse even further. All other forms of education are reduced to minor problems of other institutions, although in fact the public schools have, over time, assumed a certain amount of responsibility for those forms as well.

However, in none of these mainstream discourses of educational reform (e.g., Bennett, 1992; Hirsch, 1987; Ravitch, 1985) is the notion of a broader, inherited, colonial Puritan function of education as a spiritual quest seriously discussed. Instead, a generalized Protestantism is implied, understood and lived as a synthesis of democratic capitalism and sacred and spiritual notions (Stivers, 1994).

However, other voices have emerged to counter the prevailing view of education, a perspective that sees education, in effect, as a technical and behavioral problem in how to best transmit knowledge and produce a sense of self-control in students that will conform to moral conventions. For curriculum theorists participating in a very old discourse, retrieved in part from a Puritan heritage, the topic of morality and spirituality in relation to the purpose of American schools has become an overriding concern in need of public exploration. For Huebner (1995, 1996, 1998) and Purpel (1989), who have written extensively on this subject, the discussion is to amplify again the notion of education as a moral and spiritual activity. And, in effect, they both understand the necessity to "retrieve" a different, nontechnical language by which to discuss these aspects of education as originally given by the Puritans. However, both also place their faith in perpetuating the moral imperative and the symbols that constitute America and America's vision—the errand into the wilderness—within the boundaries of schools.

EDUCATION AS SPIRITUAL QUEST: RECOVERING A PURITAN ECHO TO SAVE AMERICA

Purpel (1989) detected two competing clamors in America's present age:

> I speak of two roars—the first has to do with the enormity of our present cultural, political, and economic crisis, and with it the incipient possibility of catastrophe. The second general realm of energy and excitement is in the world of ideas, which is bursting with ever increasing vitality and brilliance. (p. ix)

At the center of this cultural maelstrom is the institution of school. For Purpel (1989), the logic is simple and linear: How schooling goes, America goes:

> We are, I believe, very much in a cultural, political, and moral crisis, and hence, ipso facto, in an educational crisis. . . . I share the view that we as a culture, nation, a people . . . confront enormous and awesome threats to our most cherished notions of life. . . . [Education possesses a] broad responsibility for the state of the culture. . . . The failure of educational system is both cause and effect of a crisis in the culture's capacity to synthesize a coherent moral and spiritual order. (pp. 1, 28)

He placed in the hands of public schools the power, as well as the burden, to perform the ritual of exorcising the evil buried in the American spirit:

> I continue to have faith that education can indeed help us to overcome the demons. . . . What this means is obviously that when we talk about education, the stakes are very high—we are talking ultimately about the basic and most important questions of human existence. (pp. xi, 10)

That portion of America that must come to grips with this responsibility is none other than the middle class, in part because "the middle class has both political and economic power and increased educational potential, i.e., is in the position to inform its power with a moral and religious vision" (Purpel, 1989, p. x). Neither Purpel nor Huebner (1995, 1996, 1998) strayed from the dominant "traditionalists" assumption that schools are the ultimate battleground for cultural survival. However, Purpel's and Huebner's visions veer from the "traditionalists" in one significant way. They share a distinct sensitivity to how language creates meaning, and recognize that interpretation is crucial to preserve the symbols infusing America with imaginative power. In fact, Purpel (1989) and Huebner (1995, 1996) appropriated the term *education* in a different light, situating it outside the modern sense of schooling as it came to be understood in the late 19th century. Instead, each revived a Puritan sense of education as a moral and spiritual journey pursued by an individual to transcend his or her current state and capture a sense of "moreness" (Huebner, 1995, p. 16). An individual who agrees to depart on this moral pilgrimage goes a long way to sustain a symbolic structure infused with the power of imagination and narrative coherency. This view of education is guided by an impulse to retrieve America's original religious symbols coopted during the 19th century by those celebrating the scientific discourse for secular ends and meanings.

Huebner (1995) wrote that schools discarded the notion of education as a journey of a self moving along a path with other selves, each seeking transcendence, in favor of treating students as objects to be easily modified and processed along a hierarchical ladder of knowledge. Current educational language is not capable of providing for or expressing experiences of "moreness," a sense of relating to something more significant than any one individual. Without this experience, one is not inspired to further his or her thinking and engage in the act of interpretation:

> The bewitching language of psychology and the behavioral sciences has skewed our view of education. The language of ends and objectives, which guides educational practice and decision making, is used to depict a future state of affairs.
>
> The process whereby an individual moves from one state of being to another and develops new capacities or competencies is identified as "learning"—a term so much a part of the coin of the realm that it blocks the imagination. . . . "Learning" too quickly explains and simplifies that movement or journey. (Huebner, 1995, p. 17)

Purpel (1989) agreed. He wrote that the language of the technicists and behaviorists diminishes the process of education: "When I speak of trivialization, I refer to two major phenomena of educational discourse —its evasion or neglect of larger, more critical topics and the stress on technical rather than on social, political and moral issues" (p. 23). Huebner (1995) identified this tendency for schools to reduce moral discussion to technical problems, a framework in which the problem is parceled out into discrete bits to be analyzed and altered. The solution is always predetermined by the very logic of the educational language that frames the questions. The effect is that the notion of morality, its meanings and complexities, is not discussed at all. The ends have already been fixed:

> Another educational end is set, and another task imposed upon teachers. . . . The basic structures of the educational enterprise are not brought under question. By focusing upon the teaching of moral and ethical values, the conversation fails to identify the moral and ethical problems created by the structures of schooling. . . . Teachers are often blind to the moral dimension of their practice because educational language tends to call attention only to those problems that can be solved technically. (p. 1)

The privileging of technical language affected the meanings of individuality and freedom as understood and furthered by the institution of public schools. For the Puritans, such concepts provided a tension on which to contemplate. It was an extreme and powerful recovery of the Puritan maxim, "form controls matter," but more dangerous than Puritans could ever dream due to the nature of the emerging "technicist" discourse. Bowers and Flinders (1990) explained how this pattern of thought operates, specifically in terms of how it emphasizes classroom control instead of individual intellectual and spiritual growth:

> [W]e . . . use the label of "technicist" to communicate the growing importance given to reducing every aspect of experience, including the dynamics of the classroom, to technique that can be rationally formulated for the purpose of improving prediction, control, and efficiency. . . . The technicist pattern of thinking, with its machine-like analogues . . . [assumes] (1) a view of the rational process as culturally neutral, (2) a view of language as a conduit, and (3) a view of learning as individually centered [as opposed to cooperatively]. (pp. 5, 9)

Such assumptions have gradually eroded the habits of interpretation crucial to the vitality of the Puritan gift of a symbolic structure perpetuated by the ritual of the jeremiad. "Technicist" discourse acknowledges no ambiguity and allows for no multiple meanings. Language is not perceived to point to "inner" experiences, but instead becomes a clear representation of reality. In effect, interpretation is not necessary. The institution of school forgot the colonial Puritan moral imperative of an individual responsible for interpreting the symbols presented in a jeremiadic ritual. An effect of this forgetting or devaluing is clear: When social conditions change, producing a need for shifts in symbolic meanings, such adjustments fail due to the lack of a flexible language to mediate the symbols for the new time and place (Stivers, 1994). The institution of schooling, instead of adjusting to the fluctuations and disruptions of time, has in fact reduced the meanings of symbols down to simple moral maxims to be transmitted to and memorized by students (Tyack, 1993). Although the jeremiad remains the American middle-class model by which to express a sense of cultural crisis, its usefulness as a tool to evoke emotion and action in others has been rendered obsolete due to the technicist discourse that controls the schools.

In other words, the object and target of jeremiads—American youth—are no longer capable of mediating the symbols. Students can only mimic the words without understanding or providing new meanings to suit the current historical context. They believe that the American symbol of freedom has transformed into something either beyond their grasp and no longer applicable, or that it is nothing more than a cynical chase for money and power.

Yet, students continue to engage in a restless, disturbed use of the language that expresses such symbols as America and the moral imperative of the errand into the wilderness. This rupture between the impulse to mediate symbols and the lack of a language to do so produces a state of high anxiety. As Whitehead (1927/1955) pointed out, humans operate in the world in meaningful ways only through a symbolic structure. However, symbols must be interpreted, not just repeated, to sustain meaning and flexibility. What has become a game of nostalgia for those employing the jeremiad forms (Stivers, 1994), for the young is a game that makes no sense as they possess no knowledge of its purpose or its rules. The gift was not delivered. Or rather, schools delivered the gift, but in a language that is nonflexible, direct, and detrimental to the ambiguity symbols must have to survive. Simply, the gift was badly mishandled and damaged on delivery. An effect, according to Huebner and Purpel, was a shift in how the concept of freedom plays out in concrete activities of life.

Purpel (1989) argued that each individual is supposed to understand that freedom not only meant a capability to do what one wanted, but also the responsibility to do what one should as determined by a moral precedent of the community or by God's silent conversation with the individual. The moral imperative is still to become a free individual. But such a state of being was conditioned upon an individual's capability to compete against others. Success against others now translates into the freedom to do what one wants depending on one's position of authority. In a sense, this means the position to control not only one's own self but one's own environment as well (again, a guiding concept emerges: form controls matter). The school, when institutionalized, operated from the beginning premise that its function was to produce citizens to compete for the rewards of freedom and individuality (as the discussion on William Torrey Harris illustrated). An individual who wins is deemed successful. Success means one is free from environmental fetters. At the same time, one is given power to create and institute an environment for others. This freedom signals the arrival of an individual who has transcended into total selfhood and self-reliance. The moral structure of competition, of sorting out individuals who deserve freedom and the privilege of making rules for others and those who deserve to defer and willingly follow the rules, was instituted and perpetuated by schools. "Freedom has come to mean license for the powerful rather than liberation of the weak; quality is seen as the privilege of competing rather than the right to dignity" (Purpel, 1989, p. 16).

In a paradoxical twist identified by Purpel, a culture of "natural freedoms" is actually constructed on a conformist sensibility. An individual must compete against others (and be measured and accounted for) or he or she can never achieve the freedom of autonomous selfhood. Purpel wrote:

> The stress on individuality is by no means free of its conformist aspect— indeed the culture demands that individuals compete, that they strive for winning over and beating others; and that achievement in a broad but ultimately bounded realm constitutes success. (1989, p. 32)

A moral imperative of competition for success has had broad implications for schools. In America, Purpel (1989) wrote, a morality passed along within the curriculum does not have to be stated. Students figure out the reward systems and requirements early on: "Students learn very quickly that the rewards that schools provide—grades, honors, recognition, affection—are conditioned upon achievement and certain behaviors of respect, obedience and docility" (p. 35).

To master this reward system of expectation and reward provides the student with the opportunity for the acquisition of material property and an individual sense of achievement and success. The system of schooling has had the effect of making it impossible for a student to function in a cooperative manner with other students. Purpel asserted that because there is a lack of reward for this kind of behavior, a student is, in effect, taught to accentuate the natural freedom aspect of individuality without an internal check on his or her desires and actions to satisfy those desires: "Individualism has come to mean greed rather than moral autonomy and community has come to be oriented around the terms of class rather than terms of humanity" (Purpel, 1989, p. 16). The notion of a common vision, of a common purpose and identity, has dissolved into individuals competing for the right to consume whatever they are told is valuable.

For Purpel and others participating in this discourse, an answer to such a fragmented and dangerous condition lay within the boundaries of public schools. Education must be broadened by all school leaders, including teachers, in a way that resurrects forgotten notions of an early American discourse, in which the sacred infuses the secular with meaning and provides a cohering vision for all living within its geographical and symbolic boundaries. These symbols are to provide not only the possibility of action, and hence the moral imperative of engaging in the spiritual pilgrimage, but also the boundaries—the internal and external checks on an individual accentuating too much natural freedom. Purpel and Ryan did not drift far from the beliefs and concerns of 19th-century educators. In what appears a repetition of Harris, they wrote that only the schools can assume the task of education in modern society and that the family can no longer shoulder the burden of education in modern society. Purpel and Ryan (1976) wrote:

> The modern American family is smaller, more isolated and more fragmented than its counterpart fifty years ago.... [O]pportunity for parents to influence moral attitudes and thinking of their children is reduced ... church attendance has dropped.... It would appear that at a time of great need for strong values and the capacity for moral thought, the institutions traditionally supporting the moral code are in a weakened position. (pp. 7, 8)

In fact, not just the school is responsible, but also one very specific location and authority most of all—the classroom and teacher. For Purpel (and one sees this in Huebner's writing as well), the teacher wraps up in the robes of a prophet and practices prophetic education, an act in which a teacher, with persistence, reminds students of the purpose of education—the quest for the sacred: "Education communities must mediate on the question of what it means to be sacred and how an education might facilitate the quest for what is holy " (Purpel, 1989, p. 78). This (re)mindful posture assumes the characteristics of a Puritan favorite, the prophet Jeremiah, who was the predecessor to the literary form of the jeremiad:

> It is important to remember that the prophetic voice is one that speaks not only to criticism, it is also a voice of transformation. . . . He begins with a message of doom; he concludes with a message of hope. . . . The prophetic imagination is concerned with an alternative society, one with sacred dimensions. (1989, pp. 81, 85)

Huebner (1996) appealed to teachers to become moral exemplars who are willing to question the morality of the current institutional system of schooling and become politically active in reforming it. Huebner seemed to expect students not to simply embody whatever moral sensibility may spill out of the curriculum, but to bring such silent assumptions into the light and examine them with the guidance of the teacher. Otherwise, teachers are powerless over the effect of the curriculum on the students, who in turn will be diminished in their ability to act morally, which is a state of existence that will guarantee the destruction of the American identity and its historical mission.

Afterword

Technology, at an advanced level . . . makes shared experiences and traditions irrelevant. Deep symbolic meaning—the meaning of life and the meaning of history—is used to interpret such experiences and traditions. When symbolic meaning loses its practical import, it survives only as nostalgia or as a game.   —*Stivers (1994, p. x)*

A QUESTION: Once a nation is defined early using certain symbolic narratives, is it possible to choose to create new ones that have no connection to the old? Or must institutions collapse and a massive break occur before a new symbolic narrative, a "natural" activity of humankind, can be produced? If Alfred North Whitehead is correct, we are symbol mongers and must create and act on narratives in order to be purposeful humans. But what happens when the language given to the young is no longer perceived as symbolic but instead a pure reflection—not representation—of reality? And what happens when moral snippets and listings of good character are passed on as self-evident and not in need of mediation?

During the last few years, nearly every state and local government has gotten involved in the morality business by creating a curriculum of "character." In almost every case, a familiar logic was followed. First, test scores are found to be flat, which is connected to the perception that individuals have lost self-control and have become too disruptive to pay attention in class. Therefore, if individual behavior is improved, silence will ensue and concentration (e.g., memorization skills) will improve. The result is believed to be higher test scores, which translates, according to this logic, into America competing and winning the economic and military world battles. Hence, develop what moral characteristics are most basic to being an American (e.g., generalized Protestantism) and develop a method by which to transmit those characteristics. Finally, enter into the schools and "teach" the administrators and teachers how to impart these characteristics most effectively.

From this rationality have come city, state, and national programmatic solutions such as "Character Counts," "Character One," "Character Education Partnership," and so on. For example, in Baton Rouge, Louisiana, where I taught high school at the time, the mayor and a committee of community leaders decided on a list of "good" moral attributes that should be taken to the schools. The list trotted out the usual suspects: punctuality, respect [for authority], sobriety, obedience, self-discipline, and honesty. Each of these notions was believed self-evident and easily transmitted without historical explanation or cultural analysis. The perception was that the students would somehow "naturally" understand these terms, memorize them, change their behavior according to this mastery, and then enter into American institutions as productive citizens.

My question to the mayor when he presented this list to our faculty was, "What do you mean with each of these words and what cultural definition did you take into consideration, for it seems that understandings of such terms are situated differently within each culture." His response, which drew applause from most of the teachers, was that everyone knows what respect means, that it has been lost by the youth of today and that in order to save our children we must instill in them respect. Believing this was problematic, I decided to test the mayor's assumptions. In one of my literature classes, I handed out a *Sports Illustrated* article about NBA star Latrell Sprewell. According to the article, Sprewell had gotten into an argument with his head coach, left the court, but came back a couple of hours later and confronted the coach. A shouting match ensued and Sprewell proceeded to choke the coach. Sprewell stated that the coach had yelled at him too much, thereby humiliating him. I introduced to my students the notions of courage and respect as moral attributes. After reading the article, in addition to a few Associated Press stories covering the incident, we discussed whether Sprewell could be characterized as courageous and whether he understood the "proper" notions of respect.

Following the mayor's logic, one would assume the students would reply that Sprewell did not possess these characteristics, for he immediately resorted to anger and violence based on what appeared a minor insult. However, my students did not agree. Nearly every one, and these were mostly poor African-American, inner-city youth, responded that Sprewell not only demonstrated courage, but also his understanding of respect and the consequences of not showing a "man" proper respect. They said Sprewell had no choice but to teach the coach a lesson, adding that the coach had no right to yell at him. For someone in a position of power to yell and expect another to listen just because he is in a position of power is the opposite of courage, my students said. To strike back and show physical dominance is the definition of courage, they said. To prove that he could physically master the coach meant that the coach had to respect Sprewell and not the other way around.

These students had a very clear understanding of what they meant and how they acted on these notions in the world. It was their reality. To tell the students that these words could actually, according to the moral powers that be, mean just the opposite made no sense to them, nor were they interested in hearing that. The voice of institutional power poured right past them, leaving no conscious marks. Yet, few recognize that the very institutions that are trying to transmit obedience and usefulness to the individual are no longer in a position to speak to the individual. Imposition, rather than recognition, of the nature of the calling to a vocation has marked the 20th-century technological mind. Modern rhetoric still speaks of curriculum as a preparation for institutional life, which translates as preparation for serving an economic function.

Institutional life can no longer promise to deliver a sense of greater purpose or meaning to the individual who, despite still possessing the impulse, has no clue of how to locate such a design. The spiritual sense of how the individual relates to cultural institutions, developed by the colonial Puritans, has been discarded. However, the impulses and the symbols that constitute this process do not seem as meaningful to the youth in schools today, inasmuch as the symbols can no longer be interpreted anew because they have been defined by a kind of technical language appropriated over the last century. Confidence in institutions as a means to provide individuals vocations and purpose has crumbled.

However, a distinct difference exists between the culturally powerful jeremiadic form and the language employed by the colonial Puritans, which functioned to mediate an understanding of the symbols that applied to that specific time and place, and the present-age jeremiads, which function to mediate nothing because the assumption is that there is nothing there to mediate, that all is self-evident and that morality is ahistorical.

Puritans had a great impulse toward method, toward finding the one best system by which each individual could best engage in the moral imperative of the errand and integrate with his or her community. However, this impulse was associated with and directed to the experience of the subjective individual. Colonial Puritans did not possess a language of technique that limited interpretation to a literalized function, although they certainly moved the language in that direction through the appropriation of Ramism as a means of schooling and a transmission of concepts. A community was always a gathering of individuals and, therefore, open to multiple interpretations as long as the meanings that emerged from those interpretations cohered around their sense of the harmony between sacred and secular.

This is not to claim that Puritans did not seek direct and clear understandings of moral dilemmas. However, they acknowledged that when language was involved, it inherently produced ambiguity. Language could only point to and mediate what God was saying. Discourse for the Puritans also generated a poetic sense of the moral imperative and symbolic existence (what Huebner, 1995, called "moreness"), which sustained an ultimate sense of mystery (Bercovitch, 1993).

The irony of the technicist linguistic structure is that it only became possible after the Protestant Reformation, when interpretation of the Bible shifted from mainly a metaphorical/symbolic activity to a literal activity of one-to-one correspondence. This form of literal reading was appropriated as a mainstream "natural" manner by which to view and understand the world. The literal was linked to technical and mechanical metaphors as the criteria for what was real and true.

Paradoxically, even though this discourse seemed to circumvent a sense of life as a metaphorical activity, at the same time it produced new wildly popular metaphors, particularly mechanical ones dependent on certain prescribed meanings of technique. The notion of technique was appropriated and transformed by bureaucratic organizations during the 19th century. Technique had historically translated into a means by which to deal with the problems that arose in material existence; a tool and not an end in itself. God and the desire for attaining visible sainthood were the ends. In the 19th century, technique became "a sense of efficiency," an end in itself (Stivers, 1994, p. 72):

Human technique as a set of objective rules and procedures reduces its recipient to an abstraction; it denies the individuality of its object. Human technique makes everyone equal by ignoring individual difference. . . . At the same time human technique denies the subjectivity of its object, it suppresses that of the subject as well. In depending upon technical procedure instead of personal experiences, one is denying one's own subjectivity. Technique respects the individuality of neither user nor recipient. . . . Finally, human technique destroys meaning.

Technique, as we have seen, is preoccupied with efficiency, with the most effective means. In other words, technique is exclusively a means of power, autonomous, with respect to moral end. Insofar as meaning arises from the collective attempt to limit and symbolize power, technique thus lacks meaning. All attempts to infuse technique with meaning are futile, for technique is not integrated into the larger culture; rather it suppresses culture, rendering symbols ephemeral. (Stivers, 1994, p. 73)

Many continue to follow the colonial Puritan gift, the impulse to speak of moral imperatives and of the need for the perpetuation and maintenance of an American national identity. However, the language put into practice in schools has strangled the ambiguity necessary to sustain the symbols as meaningful. The process of the moral imperative engaged by each individual following a path of intensive interpretation at some point converted to an instrumental motion of providing the individual with predetermined norms and goals and the universal means by which to attain those goals. Symbols and the moral practices that tied the symbols to cultural identities became ghosts. In other words, the symbols are now ephemeral.

This condition was given concreteness after several discussions with current college and high school students. The symbols came out of their mouths and their pens, but for the most part, there was no sense of a visceral, emotional response of questioning and clarifying the identity presented as American. Nor was there any indication of anyone engaging in an interpretive turn—the kind of response and process that sustained the life of symbols for the Puritans.

Students in the present age seem to possess no way of interpreting the symbols even though they mimic the words. Or, their interpretations, if one could call them that, in no way reflect the conditions of their lives or the life of the communities within which they dwell. Students repeat with reverence the morality of success, freedom, and individuality, of

America as the best nation and of the American dream. But they have no sense of how any of it relates to them as individuals, except in the most crass way of being able to "do what they wanted to do when they wanted to do it." Many years of a schooling technique bent on reducing all symbols to easily digestible fragments, with no expectation of interpretation and personal understanding, has diminished students' sense of what Huebner called "moreness" (1995, p. 15).

When students are pushed to interpret the symbols rather than repeating them as self-evident tropes, their language falters. American national identity is important for schools to teach, they say, although in the next breath they agree, for the most part, that the notion of one, unified country is not a reasonable ideal in this present age. As said before, the symbols are but ghosts without any link to these students' material world.

To a large degree, students believe that such matters as determining meaning in the world and how one should live in this world is best left to others to confront. Whitson and Stanley (1992) described this condition that many youth, and adults for that matter, appear to exist within:

> More and more we have adjusted to a culture dominated by expert opinion while our confidence in our own abilities to make complex social judgments continues to erode. As social beings, we are often reduced to what Lasch called the "minimal" self, a self preoccupied with its own survival on a daily basis and obsessed with the need to find ways to improve self-image as an end. Life appears so complex that the average person abandons political action for personal development and survival.
>
> But these efforts are doomed to failure as only the views of significant others (experts) are deemed worth considering. A culture racked with such self-doubt, anxiety, and insecurity is unlikely to promote political competence. Citizenship is reduced to surviving, following rules, and occasionally voting. (p. 58)

Answers to such a cultural dilemma proposed by political leaders seem vacuous and not applicable to students' existence. The moment students begin to contemplate meanings and effects of these symbols, their uneasiness magnifies, yet they continue with the linguistic motion as if caught in a cavernous mountain echo. The need to continue to work within a symbolic structure is so great that the students admit to a disturbing sense of fatalism. As a student in one of my high school classes finally responded in an exasperated tone: "We have no other way of talking about these things."

Where does this leave students? Sitting in classrooms and waiting to be imparted information that they no longer see as applicable to their lives and waiting for the words of America's vision to be given to them, while at the same time realizing that such symbols no longer speak to their social condition? One could speculate that these students are caught in a time transition that, for better or worse (probably both), may be taking place in America. Once symbols no longer speak to their most important target, the youth who must appropriate and give new meanings to the symbols so that such meaning-producing structures continue to supply a culture(s) with the possibilities of identity, then a period of rupture and confusion incurs.

The current circumstance, a rupture in time, points to a Shakespearean metaphor, one that offers discomfort to those who possess faith that educational, cultural, and institutional change can be engineered: Hamlet's father, the dead king of Denmark, returns as a spirit, a revenant warning that something is terribly wrong, that all lives are about to change forever. His words tremble and speak of revenge, but they also serve to baffle and mystify. Hamlet hears but has no context by which to interpret and understand and act. Instead, Hamlet is left to listen, watch, wait, and reflect. When form no longer controls matter, when a symbolic structure and the morality it produces can no longer render a visceral response from the young, and when the interpretive turn is no longer considered natural or useful, one is left to listen, watch, reflect, and wait for new, meaningful symbols to emerge—if they emerge at all.

References

Adams, H. (1974). *The education of Henry Adams.* New York: Houghton Mifflin. (Original work published 1918)

American Heritage Dictionary of the English Language (4th ed.). (2000). New York: Houghton Mifflin.

Anyon, J. (1979). Ideology and United States history textbooks. *Harvard Educational Review, 49*(4), 361–386.

Banks, J. (1988). *Multiethnic education: Theory and practice* (2nd ed.). Boston: Allyn & Bacon.

Barnhardt, R. (Ed.). (1988). *Barnhardt dictionary of etymology.* New York: The H. W. Wilson Company.

Bellah, R. (1985). *Habits of the heart.* Berkeley: University of California Press.

Bellah, R. (1995, October 17). *The moral crisis in American public life.* Speech given at Southwest Missouri State University, Springfield, MO.

Bennett, W. J. (1992). *The de-valuing of America: The fight for our culture and our children.* New York: Summit Books.

Bercovitch, S. (1975). *The Puritan origins of the American self.* New Haven: Yale University Press.

Bercovitch, S. (1978). *The American jeremiad.* Madison, WI: University of Wisconsin Press.

Bercovitch, S. (1993). *The rites of assent.* New York: Routledge, Chapman & Hall.

Bird, A. (1899). *Looking forward: A dream of the United States of the Americas in 1999.* Utica, NY: Arno Press.

Blanke, G. (1983). Puritan contributions to the rhetoric of America's world mission. In W. Herger (Ed.), *Studies in New England Puritanism* (pp. 199–233). New York: Verlag-Peter Lang.

Bloom, A. (1987). *Closing of the American mind.* New York: Random House.

Blow, S. (1910, June). In memoriam of William Torrey Harris. *Kindergarten Review, XX,* 259–260.

Blumin, S. (1991). *The emergence of the middle class: Social experience in the American city, 1760–1900.* New York. Cambridge University Press.

Bowers, C. (1987). *Elements of a post-liberal theory of education.* New York: Teachers College Press.

Bowers, C., & Flinders, D. (1990). *Responsive teaching: An ecological approach to classroom patterns of language, culture, and thought.* New York: Teachers College Press.

Brumm, U. (1970). *American thought and religious typology.* Brunswick, NJ: Rutgers University Press.

Buchanan, P. (1992, January 6). "Put America First." *The Nation, 13,* 21.

Bullough, W. (1974). *Cities and schools in the gilded age: The evolution of an urban institution.* Port Washington, NY: Kennikat Press.

Byerly, K. (1946). *Contributions of W. T. Harris to public school administration.* Unpublished PhD dissertation, University of Chicago.

Callahan, R. (1962). *Education and the cult of efficiency.* Chicago: University of Chicago Press.

Caputo, J. (1987). *Radical hermeneutics: Repetition, deconstruction and the hermeneutic project.* Bloomington and Indianapolis: Indiana University Press.

Conway, J. (1971, Winter). Women reformers and American culture, 1870–1930. *Journal of Social History, 5*(2) 164–178.

Cotton, J. (1641). *Way of life.* London: [self-published].

Counts, G. (1969). *Dare the school build a new social order?* New York: Arnd Press & *The New York Times.* (Originally published in 1932 by the John Day Co., New York, NY)

Cremins, L. (1964). *The transformation of the school: Progressivism in American education, 1867–1957.* New York: Vintage.

Cross, R. (1975). Origins of the Catholic parochial school. In J. Barnard & D. Burner (Eds.), *The American experience in education* (pp. 168–183). New York: New Viewpoints.

Cuban, L., & Shipps, D. (2000). *Reconstructing the common good in education.* Stanford, CA: Stanford University Press.

Curti, M. (1959). *The social ideas of American educators.* Paterson, NJ: Littlefield Adams.

Dawson, W. (1984). *The unusable past.* Chico, CA: The Free Press.

Derrida, J. (1973). *Speech and phenomena* (David B. Allison, Trans.). Evanston: Northwestern University Press.

Dole, R. (1996, August). Text of Dole's speech accepting Republican nomination for president. Online: www.pbs.org/newshour/conventions96/floor_speeches/bob_dole.html

Doll, W. (1993). *A post-modern perspective of curriculum.* Columbia, NY: Teacher College Press.

Doll, W., Jr. (1998). Curriculum and the concepts of control. In W. F. Pinar (Ed.), *Curriculum: New identities in/for the field* (pp. 295–324). New York: Garland.

Dutton, B. (1889). *Discipline in the elementary school*. Address at National Education Association conference, pp. 487–488, Washington, DC.

Edwards, J. (1999). Sinners in the hands of an angry God. In *American sermons: The Pilgrims to Martin Luther King* (pp. 347–365). New York: Literary Classics of the United States. (Original work published 1740)

Eisenstein, E. (1993). *The printing revolution of early modern Europe. Canto edition*. New York: Cambridge University Press.

Ellis, M. (2001). *Revisionism in U.S. education: A historical inquiry, contemporary perspective and future prediction*. Online: www.lhup.edu/library/InternationalReview/revision.htm, Lochaven University, Internet.

Emerson, E. (1977). *Puritanism in America, 1620–1750*. Boston: Twayne.

Finn, C. (1991). *We must take charge: Our schools and our future*. New York: Free Press.

Gadamer, H.-G. (1993). *Truth and method* (2nd rev. ed.). New York: Continuum.

Geertz, C. (1973). *The interpretation of culture; selected essays*. New York: Basic Books.

Gerhard, W. P. (1900, December). A plea for rain baths in the public schools. *Journal of Social Science, 38,* 117–133.

Gillette, K. (1976). *The human drift*. Delamar, NY: Scholar's Facsimiles & Reprints. (Original work published 1894)

Greaves, R. (1969). *The Puritan revolution and educational thought: Background for reform*. New Brunswick, NJ: Rutgers University Press.

Greven, P. (1977). *The Protestant temperament*. New York: Alfred A. Knopf.

Grob, G., & Billias, G. (1972). *From Puritanism to the first party system*. New York: The Free Press.

Haller, W. (1957). *The rise of Puritanism: The way to the new Jerusalem as set forth in pulpit and press from Thomas Cartwright to John Lilburne and John Milton, 1570–1643*. New York: Harper Torch Books.

Hamilton, D. (1990). *Curriculum history*. Geelong, Victoria: Deakin University Press.

Harris, W. T. (1871, January). Nature versus human nature, or the spiritual. *American Journal of Education, 3,* 4–5.

Harris, W. T. (1874). *A statement of the theory of education in the United States of America as approved by many leading educators*. Washington, DC: U.S. Government Printing Office.

Harris, W. T. (1876). Culture and discipline versus information and dexterity. *Western, II,* 17–31.

Harris, W. T. (1877). Words versus things: The importance of language. *Western, 3,* 127–134.

Harris, W. T. (1881, September). The church, the state and the school. *North American Review, 133*, 215–227.

Harris, W. T. (1882). Education of the family and education of the school. *Journal of Social Science, XV*, 4–10.

Harris, W. T. (1883a, May). Moral education in the common schools. *Journal of Social Science, XVIII*, 122–134.

Harris, W. T. (1883b, May). Does the common school educate children above the station they are expected to occupy in life? *Education, 1*, 461–475.

Harris, W. T. (1883c, September). Moral education in schools: Report of committee on moral education to the national council of education. *Education, 5*, 1–13.

Harris, W. T. (1884, May). Moral education in common schools. *Journal of Social Science, 18*, 122–134.

Harris, W. T. (1885a). Psychological inquiry. *Education, 6*, 156–168.

Harris, W. T. (1885b, April). Immortality of the individual. *Journal of Speculative Philosophy, XIX*, 189–219.

Harris, W. T. (1885c, May). Educational need of urban civilization. *Education, 5*, 443–453.

Harris, W. T. (1886, August). How I was educated. *Forum, I*, 552–561.

Harris, W. T. (1887, April). Books that have helped me. *Forum, 3*, 142–151.

Harris, W. T. (1888a, March). The present need of moral training in public schools. *Journal of Education, XXVII*, 122–135.

Harris, W. T. (1888b, December). Excessive help in education. *Education, 9*, 215–220.

Harris, W. T. (1889a, February). Our public schools: Can morality by taught without sectarianism. *Journal of Education, XXIX*, 29–30.

Harris, W. T. (1889b, March). The present need of moral training in the public schools. *Journal of Education, XXIX*, 131–132.

Harris, W. T. (1899). An educational policy for our new possessions. *Educational Review, XVIII*, 105–118.

Harris, W. T. (1901). *Psychological foundations of education.* New York: D. Appleton.

Harris, W. T. (1902, October). How the school strengthens the individuality of the pupil. *Educational Review, XXIV*, 228–237.

Harris, W. T. (1903, July). The kindergarten as a preparation for the highest civilization. *Atlantic Educational Journal, VI*, 35–36.

Harris, W. T. (1905, January). Social culture in the form of education and religion. *Educational Review, 29*, 18–37.

Hartoonian, M. (1996). President's message. Washington, DC: National Council for the Social Studies.

Heimert, A. (1953, September). Puritanism, the wilderness, and the frontier. *The New England Quarterly, XXVI*(3), 361–382.

Higham, J. (1984). *Send these to me* (Rev. ed.). Baltimore: Johns Hopkins Press.

Higham, J. (1990). *History: Professional scholarship in America*. Baltimore: John Hopkins University Press.

Hirsch, E. D. (1987). *Cultural literacy: What every American needs to know*. Boston: Houghton & Mifflin.

Hofstadter, R. (1959). *Social Darwinism in American thought* (Rev. ed.). New York: George Braziller.

Hofstadter, R. (1962). *Anti-intellectualism in American life*. New York: Random House.

Huebner, D. (1995). Education and spirituality. *Journal of Curriculum Theory, 11*(2), 13–35.

Huebner, D. (1996). *Teaching as moral activity*. An extended version of a paper delivered at the Summer Institute on Teaching, Teachers College, Columbia University, July 8, 1990.

Huebner, D. (1998). *The lure of the transcendent: Collected essays*. Mahwah, NJ: Lawrence Erlbaum Associates.

Katz, M. (1975). *Class, bureaucracy and schools*. New York: Praeger.

Katz, M. (1987). *Reconstructing American education*. Cambridge, MA: Harvard University Press.

Kaestle, C. (1984). Moral education and common schools in America: A historian's view. *Journal of Moral Education, 13*(2), 101–111.

Kaufmann, M. (1999). *Institutional individualism: Conversion, exile, and nostalgia in Puritan New England*. London: Wesleyan University Press.

Kemp. J. (1996, August 15). Acceptance speech of Republican nomination for vice-president. http://www.pbs.org/newshour/convention96/floor_speeches/kemp.html

Kliebard, H. (1987). *The struggle for the American curriculum, 1893–1958*. Boston: Routledge & Kegan Paul.

Kliebard, H. (1992). *Forging the American curriculum*. New York: Routledge.

Leverenz, D. (1980). *The language of Puritan feeling*. Brunswick, NJ: Rutgers University Press.

Lewis, R. W. B. (1955). *The American Adam*. Chicago: University of Chicago Press.

Linn, S. P. (Ed.). (1883). *Words that burn*. Philadelphia: J. H. Chambers.

Lyons, R. (1964). *The influence of Hegel on the philosophy of education of William Torrey Harris*. Unpublished dissertation, Boston University Graduate School, Boston, MA.

Maier, P. (1997). *American scripture: Making the Declaration of Independence*. New York: Alfred A. Knopf.

Mages, M. (1999). *Magnalia christi Americana: America's literary old testament*. San Francisco: International Scholars Text.

Mather, C. (1977). *Magnalia christi americana*, Books I & II. (K. B. Murdock,

Ed.). Cambridge, MA: Harvard University Press. (Original work published 1702)

McCarthy, C. (1994). Multicultural discourses and curriculum reform: A critical perspective. *Educational Theory, 44*(1). Online: www.ed.uiuc.edu/EPS/Educational-Theory/contents/44_1_McCarthy.asp

McDannel, C. (1986). *The Christian home in Victorian America, 1840–1900.* Bloomington and Indianapolis: Indiana University Press.

Mead, S. (1977). Denominationalism: The shape of Protestantism in America. In R. Richey (Ed.), *Denominationalism* (pp. 70–105). Nashville, TN: Parthenon Press.

Miller, P. (1953). *The New England mind: From province to colony.* Cambridge, MA: Belknap Press, Harvard.

Miller, P. (1957). *Errand into the wilderness.* Cambridge, MA: Belknap Press, Harvard.

Morgan, E. (1944). *The Puritan family: Essays on religion and domestic relations in seventeenth-century New England.* Boston: Trustees of the Public Library.

Morgan, E. (1958). *The Puritan dilemma.* New York: Little, Brown.

Morgan, J. (1988). *Godly learning: Puritan attitudes towards reason, learning and education, 1560–1640.* Cambridge: Cambridge University Press.

Morison, S. E. (1936). *Three centuries of Harvard 1636–1936.* Cambridge, MA: The Belknap Press of Harvard University Press.

Mosier, R. (1956, April). Hegelianism in American education. *Educational Theory, III*(2), 97–103.

Mowry, W. (1886). Moral instruction in the public school. *Journal of Education, 23*, 75–76.

Nash, G. (1993, July). Multiculturalism and history: Historical perceptions and present projects. In D. Ravitch & M. Vinovskis (Eds.), *Historical perspectives on current education reforms* (pp. 238–262). Washington, DC: Office of Research in Office of Research and Improvement, U.S. Department of Education.

Niebuhr, R. (1966). Institutionalization and secularization of the kingdom. In R. Richey (Ed.), *Denominationalism* (pp. 145–169). Nashville, TN: Parthenon Press.

Noble, D. (1965). *Historians against history.* Minneapolis: University of Minnesota Press.

Novik, P. (1988). *That Noble dream: The "objectivity question" and the American historical profession.* Cambridge: Cambridge University Press.

Oakes, U. (1673). *New England pleaded with.* Cambridge, MA: [self-published].

Ong, W. (1958). *Ramus, method and the decay of dialogue.* Cambridge: Harvard University Press.

Ong, W. J. (1971). *Rhetoric, romance, and technology: Studies in the interaction of expression and culture.* Ithaca, NY: Cornell University Press.

Percy, W. (1991). *Signposts in a strange land.* New York: The Noonday Press.

Perkinson, H. (1991). *The imperfect panacea: American faith in education, 1865–1990* (3rd ed.). New York: McGraw Hill.

Perry, R. (1944). *Puritanism and democracy.* New York: Vanguard Press.

Pinar, W., Reynolds, W., Slattery, P., & Taubman, P. (1995). *Understanding curriculum.* New York: Peter Lang.

Purpel, D. (1989). *The moral & spiritual crisis in education: A curriculum for justice & compassion in education.* New York: Bergin and Garvey.

Purpel, D., & Ryan, K. (1976). *Moral education . . . it comes with the territory.* Berkeley, CA: McCutchan.

Ravitch, D. (1985). *The schools we deserve: Reflections on the educational crisis of our time.* New York: Basic Books.

Ravitch, D. (2000). *Left back: A century of failed school reform.* New York: Simon & Schuster.

Rorty, R. (1976, July). Realism and reference. *Monist, 59,* 321–340.

Rotundo, A. (1987). Learning about manhood: gender ideals and the middle-class family in nineteenth century America. In J. Mangan & J. Walvin (Eds.), *Manliness and morality: Middle-class masculinity in Britain and America, 1800–1940* (pp. 35–51). New York: St. Martins Press.

Sadovnik, A., Cookson, W., & Semel, S. (2001). *Exporing education: Introduction to the foundations of education* (2nd ed.). Boston: Allyn and Bacon.

Schlesinger, A., Jr. (1991a). *Disuniting of America.* New York: WW Norton & Company.

Schlesinger, A., Jr. (1991b). The disuniting of America. *American Educator, 15*(3), 21–33.

Scholes, R. (1989). *Protocols of reading.* New Haven, CT: Yale University Press.

Schwartz, S. (2001). The origins of history's mission in American schools: A case study of Hannah Adams. *Theory and Research in Social Education 29*(2), 212–237.

Scott, D. H. (2000) A vision of veritas: What Christian scholarship can learn from the Puritans' "technology" of integrating truth. *Origins.* Online: http://www.origins.org/aip/docs/scott.html

Shapiro, H. S., & Purpel, D. E. (Eds.). (1993). *Critical social issues in American education: Toward the 21st century.* White Plains, NY: State College.

Spring, J. (1972). *Education and the rise of the corporate state.* Boston, MA: Beacon Press.

Spring, J. (1986). *The American School, 1642–1985.* New York: Longman.

Spring, J. (1989). *The sorting machine revisited: National educational policy since 1945.* New York: Longman.

Stearns, P. (1987). Men, boys and anger in American society, 1860–1940. In J. Mangan & J. Walvin (Eds.) *Manliness and morality: Middle-class masculinity in Britain and America, 1800–1940* (pp. 75–92). New York: St. Martins Press.

Stivers, R. (1994). *The culture of cynicism: American morality in decline.* Cambridge, MA: Blackwell.

Stone, L. (1979) *The family, sex and marriage in England, 1500–1800* (Abridged ed.). New York: Harper Torchbooks.

Tanner, D. (1991). *Crusade for democracy: Progressive education at the crossroads.* Albany, NY: State University of New York Press.

Tanner, L. (1982). Curriculum history as usable knowledge. *Curriculum Inquiry, 12*(4), 405–412.

Tanner, D., & Tanner, L. (1980). *History of the school curriculum.* New York: Macmillan.

Taylor, C. (1975). *Hegel.* Cambridge: Cambridge University Press.

Taylor, H. L. (1892, October). American childhood from a medical standpoint. *Journal of Social Science, 30,* 44–55.

Troen, S. (1975). *The public and the schools: Shaping the St. Louis System, 1838–1920.* Columbia: University of Missouri Press.

Tyack, D. (1974). *The one best system: A history of American urban education.* Cambridge, MA: Harvard University Press.

Tyack, D. (1975). Bureaucracy and the common school: The experience of Portland, Oregon, 1851–1913. In J. Barnard & D. Burner (Eds.), *The American experience in education* (pp. 145–167). New York: New Viewpoints.

Tyack, D. (July, 1993). Reinventing schooling: Utopian impulse and historical scorecard. In D. Ravitch & M. Vinovskis (Eds.), *Historical perspectives on current education reforms* (pp. 336–384). Washington, DC: Office of Research in Office of Research and Improvement, U.S. Department of Education.

Tyack, D., & Hansot, E. (1982). *Managers of virtue: Public school leaders in America: 1820–1980.* New York: Basic Books.

Von Rad, G. (1967). *The message of the prophets.* San Francisco: Harper.

Weeks, J. (1993). *Against nature: Essays on history, sexuality and identity.* Concorde, MA: Paul and Co.

Webster's New College Dictionary, II. (1995). New York: Houghton Mifflin.

Welter, R. (1962). *Popular education and democratic thought in America.* New York: Columbia University Press.

Westbury, I. (1999). Teaching as a reflective practice: What might *didaktik* teach curriculum. In I. Westbury, S. Hopmann, & K. Riquarts (Eds.), *Teaching as a reflective practice: The German didactic tradition* (pp. 15–39). Mahwah, NJ: Lawrence Erlbaum Associates.

What matters most: Teaching for America's future (1996, September). Report of the national commission on teaching & America's future. New York: National Commission on Teaching & America's Future.

White, D. (1969, April). Education in the turn-of-the-century city: The search for control. *Urban Education, 4*(1), 169–182.

Whitehead, A. (1955). *Symbolism: Its meaning and effect.* New York: G. P. Putnam's Sons. (Original work published 1927)

Whitson, A., & Stanley, W. (1992). Citizenship as practical competence. *International Journal of Social Education, 7*(2), 57–66.

Wiebe, R. (1967). *The search for order.* New York: Hill and Wang.

Wiebe, R. (1969). The social function of public education. *American Quarterly, 21*(2), 147–165.

Williams, R. (1983). *Keywords: A vocabulary of culture and society* (Rev. ed.). New York: Oxford University Press.

Willie, C. (1992). Multiculturalism bashing: A review of magazine coverage. *Change, 24*(1), 70–75.

Winthrop, J. (1958). Christian charitie: A model hereof. In E. Morgan (Ed.), *Puritan political ideas: 1558–1794* (pp. 77–93). New York: Bobbs-Merrill. (Original work published 1630)

Wittgenstein, L. (1973). *Philosophical investigations* (G.E.M. Angcombe, Trans.). New York: Macmillan.

Wood, G. (1992). *The radicalism of the American revolution.* New York: Alfred A. Knopf.

Wuthnow, (1989). *Meaning and moral order.* Berkeley, CA.: University of California Press.

Young, E. F. (1902). *Ethics in the school.* Chicago: University of Chicago Press.

Zuckerman, M. (1988, December). *The contest of public culture in American since the sixties.* Paper presented at the American Historical Association annual meeting, Cincinnati, OH.

Author Index

Subject Index